The Successful Florist

The Successful Florist
A guide for beginners, staff and management

Stanley Coleman

B T Batsford Limited   London

© Stanley Coleman 1988
First published 1988

All rights reserved. No part of this publication
may be reproduced, in any form or by any means,
without permission from the Publisher

Photoset by Deltatype Ltd, Ellesmere Port, Cheshire
and printed in Great Britain by
The Bath Press Ltd
Bath, Somerset
for the publishers
B T Batsford Limited
4 Fitzhardinge Street
London W1H 0AH

British Library Cataloguing in Publication Data

Coleman, Stanley
   The successful florist: a guide for
beginners, staff and management.
   1. Florists — Great Britain
   I. Title
   381′.456359′0941   SB443.4.G7

ISBN 0-7134-5865-8

Contents

Acknowledgment 8
The Flower Industry 9

Part 1　The makings of a florist 13

Training 14
Finance 15
　Trading accounts 15
　Value Added Tax (VAT) 16
　Gross profit 17
　Choosing an accountant 17
　Mark-up 18
　Accounts 18
Finding suitable premises 22
　Trading from home 24
　Running a franchise 25
　The flower kiosk 25
　Locating a shop 25
　Ideal premises 26
Equipping the shop 27
Staffing 29
Insurance 29
Legal notices 29
Daily operations in a flower shop 30
　Conditioning cut flowers and plants 31
　Buying 33
　Flower relay 33

Part 2 The year round 35

Seasonal flowers 42
  Spring 42
  Summer 45
  Autumn 49
  Christmas foliages 51
Plant care 52
  On arrival 52
  Display 52
  In-store care 53
  The so-called 'poisonous' plants 53
  Bulbs and dish gardens 56
Diversifications 56
  Bedding plants and garden supplies 56
  Artificial and dried flowers 57
  Pottery and glassware 58
  Wicker and cane products 58
  Flower arranging sundries 58
  Ribbons 59
  Giftware 59
  Cards 60
  Books 60
  Toys 60

Part 3 Sales force in floristry 61

Sales staff – who are they? 61
  Responsibility 62
  Confidence 62
  Look in the mirror 63
  Personal appearance 64
  Qualifications 65

Preparedness 66
Self-confidence 67
Selling floristry 68
Wedding orders 72
Funeral orders 76
Relay orders 78
Selling by telephone 80
Care and rotation of stock 83
Servicing the stock 84
Packaging and wrapping 93
Card care 95
Cash and credit 96
Complaints 98
The individual touch 99

Part 4 Management 101

Display 103
  Windows 104
  Lighting 105
The sales area 106
  Flexibility 106
  Pride and prejudice 106
  Key points 107
  Display space 108
  Cash control 110
  Wrapping and packing area 110
  Access and movement 111
  Oil on the wheels 112
  The immovable objects 113
  Documentation 117
Peaks and bottlenecks 122
  Planning 125
Buying 127
Marketing, publicity and advertising 132

The product 135
  Quality 135
  Availability of supplies 136
  Unit sizes, unit packs and unit prices 137
  The potential field of sale 138
Finance 140
  Gross profit, overheads and net profit 141
  Mark-up 141
  Evaluation of workroom costs 144
  Pension schemes 145

Appendix Safety in the shop 147
  Premises 147
  Built-in hazards 147
  Fire hazards 148
  Electrical hazards 148
  General 148

Index 151

Acknowledgment

I would like to thank: Jack Gillet FRPI, AMIBF, MITD, of Southwark College; Mike and Janice Cotterell, of Cirencester and Bourton-on-the-Water; Martin and Shirley Cocks, of Newent; Messrs Sutch Florists' Cards, of Sevenoaks, Kent; Vanessa Coleman, for illustrations; Jacqueline Elgood, for proof-reading; Rona Coleman, for patience; Captain Bouchard for a sea-voyage, when the first draft of this book was written.

Redmarley 1988 SC

The Flower Industry

For millions of years the plant life of this planet has been developing. As with the animal kingdom, there is no doubt that some species prospered for a period and then either died out entirely, or adapted themselves to changes of environment. The development of a species was by natural selection: the winds, the waters, the animals and insects all played their part.

Man evolved and needed plant life for food, and very soon found pleasure in the ornamental nature of the vegetation around him. Early civilisations used flowers and foliages in decoration, for ritual or religious purposes and for personal adornment. The habit continued albeit with some breaks in continuity as great empires rose and fell. The cultivation of plants and herbs by the Romans, for example, was advanced, and without doubt assumed business proportions in this country as well as in Europe. But the Romans departed and from the Dark Ages right up until the eighteenth century, plant and flower cultivation was in the hands of the privileged few: the houses and castles of the rich, the manor houses, the religious orders, and the royal households. However, Man's inquisitive nature – a desire to learn and record knowledge – was beginning to break through. Gerard's *Herball* completed early in the seventeenth century is a magnificent accumulation of fact and fable about plant life, and the illustrations and sensitive descriptions of both flowers and fruits are models for all ages. The expansion of scientific research and plant knowledge received a tremendous boost after the Restoration of the Monarchy and, in the years following, the Royal Society and the Horticultural Society were formed. Simultaneously, the skills of cultivation were more universally understood and used. Gardens, even cottage gardens, could boast more than the flowers bequeathed by nature, and 'gardeners' became recognised as such and began to 'garden' commercially.

However, there was the problem that flowers had a short life whether grown in the open, or under the early glasshouses, and if they were to be sold in the cities, needed to be transported there quickly. Growers near to London could send produce to Covent Garden with their fruit and vegetables on the great horse-drawn drays. Market gardeners along the south side of the Thames would carry their produce into the market. The volume and nature of the flowers sold in the 1840s is recorded in great detail in Mayhew's *London Labour and the London Poor*. It is significant that the bulk of the flowers recorded as passing through the market are sold by street traders in this period.

With the railway came great changes. No longer were the more distant growers separated from the big cities. They could get their produce into the market within hours; what is more, they could go themselves and sell. For the markets, and particularly Covent Garden, there were reciprocal advantages. Perishable produce could not only be sent to the market, but also sent from, and over greater distances than ever before.

There was a multitude of growers, thus it was not long before one grower-salesman would be selling produce on behalf of one or more others, and receiving a commission on his sales. From this, the first of the commission-salesmen appeared, and many firms that are now famous names in the markets of the country had their beginnings in the latter half of the last century.

The retailing of flowers took on a new importance. Steady supplies and a wider range of varieties encouraged the development of flower shops. Previously retailing had been largely in the hands of the street traders with a few centrally situated stores offering flowers and a floristry service. It became possible for the street trader to seek permanent premises, and the fruiterer who sold a few flowers to become a 100% flower shop. Some shops were the development of small nurseries, or 'gardens' – others were a logical progression by firms already noted for the quality of their products and services.

Science and botanical exploration had not stood still, and the enquiring minds of the sixteenth and seventeenth centuries had led the way to steady research and exploration. Plant-hunters brought back specimens from the other side of the globe and Darwin came back and shook the establishment with his theories of evolution. All of this provided a backing of scientific knowledge and biological understanding of plants and of plant life to an expanding industry. It was in this period that the Floral Hall (looking a little like a small Crystal Palace) and the Flower Market Hall were built in Covent Garden.

Pure floristry, as we know it today, found its natural outlet and stimulus through the flower shop. Floristry skills had developed through the ages. Indeed one early writer describes a florist as one who is 'skilled with flowers'. The early florists were more likely to have been maid-servants, house-keepers, gardeners; people employed in another capacity but with certain artistry and skills that were called into use when needed. With the changes that came in the last century, many of these became the first of the florists as we know them today. Art and techniques had to develop side by side. There were no schools, no training facilities, and the techniques were passed on, person to person. 'Stand there and watch Nelly' was the kind of start that many a youngster could expect. Some of us can still remember such instructions.

So, distribution and selling of flowers became a healthy industry, related to and running alongside edible horticulture and the world of market gardening, but with strength enough to stand on its own feet and to specialise in the sale of flowers and floristry.

In Britain, florists' shops tend to be relatively small businesses, owned and run very often by a family. On average two or three staff are employed but busy city shops employ many more, whilst in country areas the shop may be run entirely on family labour. There is ample room for individuality, enterprise and skill, but such attributes are worthless without a clear understanding of the economics of business management, and an appreciation of the obligations and risks which must be embraced by those who trade in perishable produce.

Part 1 of this book is a guide principally for the inexperienced, but should be helpful to many already in business as a standard check upon existing procedures.

Part 2 gives a picture of the year-round supply position, of buying and the in-store treatment of goods. The principal varieties of flowers and plants are discussed in detail, and there are general hints that would apply to all of the produce likely to be sold in a flower shop.

Part 3 presents a salesmanship course for staff and for all those entering the trade without previous experience.

Part 4 is for proprietors and managers. By question and suggestion it is intended to help all who find themselves in charge of a retail flower shop. It is recognised that some of the advice given in this section is controversial, but the prime intention is to encourage thought and perhaps a degree of self-assessment.

PART ONE

The makings of a florist

Within reason, age is not important. Some people begin at 14, working perhaps as a Saturday hand, others come into the trade much later, and many stay in it for the whole of their working lives.

Health, however, is important. Floristry is not a sitting-down job and much time will be spent on your feet. One must be prepared to handle damp and sometimes cold materials without flinching, and be able to carry reasonably heavy loads. Those who suffer from asthma or a skin allergy should take medical advice before entering the flower industry, for all too often such problems are intensified by contact with flowers, foliages and pollen. Those with previous business experience outside floristry can often come in with a strong advantage. But it is rare to be able to run a business without direct contact with the flowers and with floristry. Training in and/or understanding of floristry design is essential for all who would own or manage a florist's shop.

Florists enter the industry in a number of different ways. For example, sons and daughters of established florists often grow up with the trade and carry on the business after their parents have retired. Others, however, may enter the trade by taking employment with a florist and obtaining their training as they work. Yet another group obtain their training before becoming fully employed or taking over a business. City and Guilds (now National Examinations Board) qualifications give a sound basis of training, though a National Diploma should be sought by all who have the necessary preliminary qualifications. Short courses are available for those entering the industry later in life and are absolutely essential for those intending to open a retail shop. Finally, in the high risk area, there are those who take the plunge with neither training nor experience. Only the lucky ones survive.

Training

Before opening a business, both training and experience are necessary. Those fortunate enough to have taken a National Diploma course such as is offered currently at the Welsh College of Horticulture, can enter the industry with a solid basis of both. Others may take employment as trainees and become trained under a day-release scheme, or perhaps an intensive course at one of the many centres offering floristry.

An alternative is to take a short intensive course of training before seeking experience by working as a member of staff for an established florist. Variations, or combinations of the above possiblities may apply in family businesses.

The majority of flower shops are 'florists' in the wide sense of the word, offering a range of flowers, plants and accessories, all kinds of floristry and, usually, flower relay facilities. Besides these, however, there are the shops, kiosks and 'departments' which specialise in the quick sale of flowers and plants, usually on a cash and carry basis. Even so, they require the same quick and intelligent sales staff as are needed throughout the industry. Experience in either type of outlet can be of immense value, but it must be understood that one cannot claim to be a florist without a clear understanding and ability to create designs with flowers. Everyone coming into the trade should be prepared to train and to seek the accepted floristry qualifications.

Note
Currently the highest qualification obtainable in Britain is the National Diploma of the Society of Floristry. The Welsh College of Horticulture offers a three-year course towards a National Diploma under B/TEC syllabus. The Intermediate Diploma of the Society of Floristry is a step towards the National Diploma, as are the four graded examinations organised by the National Examination Board.

Full information may be obtained from:
The Secretary, The Society of Floristry, The Old Schoolhouse, Payford, Redmarley, Gloucestershire GL19 3HY.
The National Examinations Board, c/o City and Guilds of London Institute, 46 Britannia Street, London, WC1X 9RG.
The Principal, The Welsh College of Horticulture, Northop, nr Mold, Clwyd.

Finance

Opening a business requires capital. Investment of capital may be from your own resources or as a loan or perhaps a mortgage upon another property. Either way, it is an investment and should be evaluated as such, and the business which it has helped to found should pay back reasonable interest, at least in line with the amount that capital might have earned if invested elsewhere.

Most shops are individually owned. Partnerships are not generally advisable and if others are involved initially with the investment, Limited Company status is preferable. Your accountant will advise you upon the steps necessary to form such a Company.

Trading accounts

Proper records of trading must be kept for Income Tax and VAT purposes. Your accountant will need these in order to prepare your trading accounts for the year. Essential books are:

    a 'Bought' ledger, preferably with space for double entry analysis columns
    a 'Sales' Ledger, with space for cash and credit analysis
    a VAT records book or file
    a credit account ledger (or file)
    bank file
    staff wages and records book.

In opening a new business it will be helpful if you keep a clear and separate record of costs involved in the founding of the business, ie property cost, lease, initial rentals, equipment, repairs and decorations, lighting, plumbing and flooring. Your accountant will need this information when negotiating your Tax liabilities in your first years in business.

File all invoices and receipts carefully, even those little 'cash paid' slips that are issued in supermarkets and DIY stores. Your accountant will advise you as to how long they need to be kept, and upon any questions relating to Value Added Tax.

In the first few weeks of trading you will need a cushion of ready cash for the unforeseen items. Be prepared for this. It is over and above the amount you will be spending upon initially stocking the shop.

Value Added Tax

A small business, with turnover under £21,000 per annum, is not required to be registered for VAT. But if you are in business, then as soon as your turnover (not just profit) exceeds the stated annual rate (currently £21,300) you should make contact at once with your local VAT office. The address and telephone number may be found in the telephone book, under the heading Customs and Excise. The officers are very willing to advise, and you will find that the following booklets are informative: 700/1/86 (retail schemes), 727/1/83 (for Teleflorist members), 727/2/83 (for Interflora members) and, most useful of all if you are new to VAT, the booklet entitled *Should I be registered for VAT?*

Initially it will look very complicated, but once you have become used to the system it becomes a simple extension of your normal recording and accounting method. If in any doubt you should ask the advice of your accountant.

It must be remembered that your VAT liability is a legal charge upon your business, but is in no way a part of your business. Within the common law of this country you are free to trade in your own way. You may buy and sell at prices which are appropriate to your style of trading. VAT law requires only that you pay VAT upon your purchases and charge VAT upon your sales, remitting the balance, quarterly, to Customs and Excise, using form VAT 100.

In smaller businesses, those not required (as yet) to register for VAT, the retailer must pay VAT upon the purchase price of the produce, but is not entitled to charge, nor show a VAT element in selling. It may be argued that he is free to make his own selling price, and can thus cover himself for the additional outlay. He is at a disadvantage, however, when a customer expresses a wish to have an invoice showing not just the price of the flowers, but the VAT element. The unregistered retailer cannot supply this and is breaking the law if he does so. There is therefore a marginal advantage in registering for VAT as soon as your turnover approaches the entry limit. Earlier registration is permissible in certain circumstances (see section 8 of *Should I be Registered for VAT?*).

Gross profit

Gross profit is the total amount received from the sale of goods, less the initial cost of those goods. From your gross profit you must pay for the 'overheads' of the business (rent, rates, wages, lighting, heating, etc) and the amount left afterwards is your *net profit*, (the diagram on page 21 illustrates the principle).

In a limited company it is usual for the director (or management) to be paid a salary as part of the committed overheads. In personally run businesses it is usual for the whole of the net profit to be regarded as the earned income of the proprietor(s).

Mortgage or loan interest should be regarded as a business 'overhead'. The advice of your accountant should always be obtained in presenting your trading figures to the Inspector of Taxes.

Choosing an accountant

Most people engaged in business employ the services of an accountant, and it is both prudent and logical to do so. If you do not know of one, recommendation by another retailer or small business proprietor can be very helpful. Indeed some accountants and accountancy firms specialise in advising and solving the problems of small businesses.

Mark-up

Your gross profit is obtained from your mark-up on goods sold. For example, if a bunch of flowers costs you £1, and you sell it for £1.50, you are operating a 50% mark-up. If it is sold for £2.50, you have a 150% mark-up. You have to decide whether it is wise to attempt to sell a large quantity of flowers at a low mark-up or more limited quantities (perhaps of better produce) at 150% mark-up or even higher. Such decisions depend very much upon the location of the shop, the type of customer you wish to attract, the 'style' of your trading, and perhaps other influences such as local competition, market days, etc.

To an outsider, even a 100% mark-up seems high. Growers too have been known to make adverse comment when they see their produce priced in city centre shops at seemingly unreasonable levels. Such thinking takes no account of the perishable nature of flowers, of the relatively high cost of city centre premises, the risk of damage by weather, or in transit, of shortages, variation in grading and, above all, the fickleness of public taste and preference. Whilst experience can reduce the adverse effects of the latter, the problem remains. Flowers should not be sold unless they have a reasonable vase-life and wastage is the cross that all florists have to bear. For accountancy purposes some record of wastage should be kept.

In a confidential survey of some successful city centre florists, mark-up was high, but gross profits were mostly within the bracket 46 to 66%. Cash and carry sales kiosks look for a lower mark-up (50 to 75%) and hope to clear, but they too have their problems with wastage, unless there is some sale-or-return agreement with suppliers or importers.

A skilled trader may find it possible to keep a foot in both camps and to offer high style floristry and a cash-and-carry outlet. Success or otherwise depends upon one's location and the possibility of 'passing trade'.

Accounts

Goods bought should be paid for either at once or upon a regular monthly account system agreed with the wholesaler. If you pay cash you are entitled to expect a discount. However, produce bought in a wholesale market is usually paid for in cash (or cheque) and, having perhaps had your bid accepted, a further discount is unlikely.

Credit allowed to your customers should be watched very carefully, because many businesses have gone under simply because they were owed too much money. The golden rule is 'No Credit' unless your customer can present reasonable credentials. Even these are of little help if he does eventually let you down, but a first screening will sort out the casual adventurer.

At the other end of the scale, some good accounts can go 'bad' if you operate a lax system. A few simple rules may help:

Cash with order or cash upon delivery is preferable to all forms of credit.

Receipts should be given, whenever requested, showing (if you are registered) the VAT element which is required by many companies.

If it is a credit sale, an invoice must go with the goods, or, in the case of a relay order or flowers to another person, an invoice must be rendered on the same day to the customer. You may, if you think fit, offer a discount for payment within seven days, because re-rendering with a statement can possibly cost you more than you have allowed. If unpaid within seven days, a statement must go out promptly, emphasising that the total amount shown is due upon the date at the top of the statement. If at the end of the month you have received no payment (and perhaps other items have been added) a firm reminder should go, together with a note stating closure of the credit facility. Keep copies of all documentation in case you have to go to the Small Claims court to obtain your money.

Notwithstanding the above, certain agreements may be reached with corporations or public bodies allowing longer terms of credit with utter security of payment. In your judgment you may decide that this is good business and allow such credit terms. Remember, however, that it can affect your cash flow. Credit business can look good, but it will not buy your flowers in the wholesale market, nor pay your rent.

Within the shop certain types of order, such as for wedding flowers, may produce difficulties over payment. It is not unusual for a family to overspend on bouquets and decorations, with the result

Initial costs of opening a florist's shop

TRADING ACCOUNT	STOCK IN TRADE	
CAPITAL INVESTMENT	Equipment and tools Books Display and work benches Shop fitting Vases and buckets Typewriter Cash-register	This illustrates the several essential items of expenditure which must be regarded as your primary investment in business. The proportions are *not to scale* and can vary considerably in relation to the size and nature of the proposed shop.
	Vehicle	
	Adaption of premises including: blinds water heating lighting flooring facia and window décor	
	Initial costs of lease first rental or down payment for purchase of premises	

THE MAKINGS OF A FLORIST

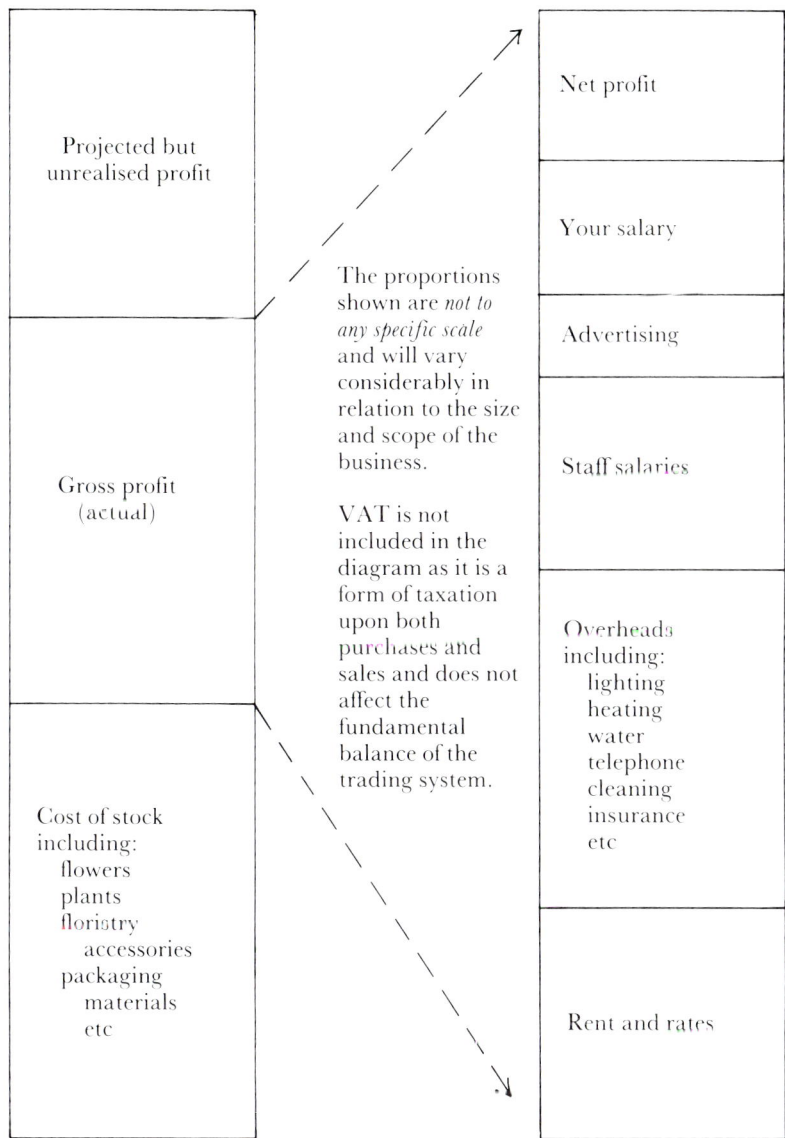

The proportions shown are *not to any specific scale* and will vary considerably in relation to the size and scope of the business.

VAT is not included in the diagram as it is a form of taxation upon both purchases and sales and does not affect the fundamental balance of the trading system.

Notes

If you own your premises, the rent is payable to you, and should reflect the amount you would expect to receive if the premises were let to another business.

A notional or peppercorn rent is not recommended and accounting should be realistic. Should you wish to sell your business in some future year, your buyer will require full accountant-certified figures for at least the previous three years of trading, and the rent is part of that comprehensive picture.

that the florist may have to wait many months for payment. Unless your customer is well-known as credit-worthy, cash with order, or at the latest upon delivery, is advisable.

Finding suitable premises

The search can be wide or narrow in scope. Personal circumstances and ambitions may point you in a certain direction and there is much to be said for doing that which your instinct tells you is right. We see many kinds of flower shops, varying widely in size, attractiveness, and in the kinds of service they offer. If your ambition is to serve a wide cross-section of the public, you must be prepared to offer the full range of flowers, plants, floristry and accessories, plus, possibly, dried materials, pottery and glassware. At the extremes you may opt for high-style floristry and gift-ware with limited sales of cut flowers, or, for a cash-and-carry flowers and plants shop in a busy market centre.

If suitable premises are located in a distant town, you will need to weigh carefully the time/cost factors in travelling to and fro, or of finding living quarters near the shop.

A comprehensive florist's shop will require more floor space than the high-style studio, or the cash-and-carry sales point, which could be a kiosk. With these broad fundamentals in mind, the search can begin. Shop premises may be located through agents, through advertisements in newspapers, or by word of mouth. You may actually see the premises you want, with the agent's name in the window, and you can begin your negotiations from there. But in your local town, gentle enquiries and local gossip may lead you to premises that have not yet been put onto the market. Sometimes news of a neglected business being offered as a going concern will circulate first in this way. If such should come your way, give it fair consideration as it could provide you with an ideal opening. Certified accounts for the last three years must be presented, however, and your accountant will advise you upon the price that you should offer.

Alternatively, you may already be in business, perhaps as a fruiterer and greengrocer, and considering extension into full-scale floristry. In the right location there is much to be said for such an extension, but it is absolutely necessary to make a clear departmental division between floristry and the sale of other produce. First, flowers and fruit do not mix well in a shop and the ethylene gas given off by many fruits is a killer for flowers. Then there is the problem of VAT accountancy – fruit and vegetables are not (currently) subject to VAT whilst flowers and plants are, and it is the total turnover of a shop which interests the VAT man. Always seek professional advice if you are contemplating sub-division within the same premises.

Over all, there is a great deal to be said for setting one's sights high; to go for a good position and to challenge the competition, to speculate and to offer a better or different service than has existed in the selected area. It will cost more than a modest beginning. The stakes are high but it has happened successfully and it will happen again. Premises will claim your biggest outlay wherever you decide to open but your estimates must allow reasonable amounts for decoration, furnishing and publicity. If competition is there you must be *seen* to compare favourably from the opening.

Out in the more rural areas, a shop as an adjunct to a nursery is valid provided the public can be made aware that it is there. Nurseries are not always on a main road, and when out of sight of the passing public the shop will get no passing trade. When on a main road, however, with clear visibility, good parking space for cars and a clearly identified shop (not a section of a greenhouse, unless cunningly disguised), a florist can operate successfully. The building need not be expensive, though you should be prepared for some re-rating if the premises have not been used for retail trading before. Consult your local authorities, too, upon entrances and the safety factor if you are on a busy road.

A variation upon this is the shop within a Garden Centre. More often than not this will be a cash-and-carry venture, possibly even a franchise, but it has one drawback. It is rarely seen at all except by those visiting the Garden Centre for other goods, and is therefore very subject to seasonal variations in trade prospects. Not recommended as a franchise but could be operated seasonally by the owners of the site.

Trading from home

This is not recommended. Having said that, we are well aware that some successful florists have started in just this way, and have later expanded into properly equipped business premises. But there have been many less happy results.

For home trading
- It is comfortable and there is less travel
- There is no obligation to be 'open' to the public
- Little or no display is necessary
- There are no costs for shop property
- Nature of business can be selective

Against home trading
- Can you obtain a reasonable return for turning over a portion of your home to business?
- Can you get a reasonable return for your time and expertise? (difficult to assess unless you are only doing it for pin-money) Probably NO.
- Supplies can be a problem. Most wholesalers are not willing to trade with 'amateurs' or those with no true stake in the industry. Neither are you likely to be popular with your local florist with whom you will be taking an unfair advantage by operating as a florist with no real business commitment.
- Local authorities do not smile upon those who conduct businesses from private houses. Once your activities are known you will most likely be re-rated.

Floristry is a *living* for many people in all sections of the industry. Hence those who operate on the fringe are not likely to be popular. There is nothing wrong with 'doing your own flowers', but doing flowers for others, for payment, is seen as an 'under the counter' activity.

Running a franchise

Running a franchise within a store or supermarket requires:
(a) Sound experience of running a flower shop.
(b) Discipline. The conditions of the franchise must be observed to the letter.
(c) Care and legal advice over the Agreement which will be required before you can operate. Study particularly the obligatory hours of trading, chargeable overheads, financial obligations, especially those relating to percentages of net profit or of gross turnover. A franchise can work, but care is needed. Never plunge into one without experience and professional advice.

The flower kiosk

The kiosk is simply a selling point for flowers and, probably, plants; items that can be carried away and paid for in cash. Product knowledge, display aptitude and selling ability are prime requirements. Floristry rarely comes into the scene. Some such selling points are operated as part of a chain, whilst others are run as a branch, or branches of an established florist. The occasional roadside kiosk or stall may be independently operated. Such selling points can be profitable as they require minimum staff, but some back-up is necessary in terms of storage and (unless run from a nursery) transport. Not recommended without experience and understanding of the industry.

Locating a shop

To succeed in business you must become *known*. You will become known more quickly if you are *seen*. Seen, that is, by those whom you hope will become your customers.

Thus a primary site is to be preferred, such as in a main shopping street or centre, a High Street, or in a nearby situation through which many people will pass on foot. (The route to and from a car park or bus station can offer a prime position.)

A secondary situation is off the main street, perhaps where it begins to taper into domestic development, or in a place close to the best shopping area but not attracting as many pedestrians. The overhead costs of a secondary site are usually well below those of the primary, but this is where you must be careful for there is no distinct line between the two, and agents have been known to have lively imaginations about the shopping potentials of some very secondary sites.

Consider the town, the shops already there and flourishing, and those that are not, also the shoppers: are they all locals or do they come in from surrounding districts? (Many a small town has a wide and useful catchment area, whilst another may have lost its commercial viability to another more lively town.) This can only be studied on foot and by observing the movement of people. What kind of people are they and where do they come from? Why do they pass in their hundreds along one street and not another. Those who come in by bus, where do they live? Is there a good residential area within the town, or do people retire and move away? Is there an industrial area and is it prosperous? Are you prepared to serve the surrounding area and perhaps a nearby township? All of these are questions that only you can answer, and usually only after some quiet research and observation. Plus one very important call – that to the town-planning department, to make sure that the shop you have your eye on is not destined to be demolished to make way for a by-pass or maybe a municipal car park.

Also, a question to the vendor or landlord: What trading restrictions are applied to the property? It can be embarrassing to be told after one has moved in that you may not sell, say, pottery or glassware in this shopping area as another trader is doing so and is entitled to be the sole retailer of such goods.

Ideal premises

Very few shops have built-in conditions ideal for floristry. In taking over premises, some adaptations to the needs of the trade are always required and it is not unusual for a complete re-fit to be necessary.

A comprehensive florist's shop needs, firstly, adequate display and selling space. Preferably the shop should not face south as sunshine can give very warm display window conditions. Suitable blinds must be allowed for if this is the situation. The display and selling area should occupy at least two thirds of the floor space, with the remaining one third (or less) devoted to workroom, office and toilets, etc. A packing room is an added refinement when space allows, plus a cooler, or cold room. Good lighting is vital, as is a hot and cold water supply, non-slip floor throughout and an attractive décor in pale or neutral colouring. There are other refinements that might be added, but the above are the broad outlines which should be borne in mind from the beginning.

A florist's shop does not necessarily have to be large and spreading. Many lively businesses are run from relatively small shops which have been skilfully adapted.

If time is not on your side, it would be wise to consult a specialist shopfitter who will submit plans and a clear estimate for all the work required. Possibly it will cost less using local labour, or even your own labour, but quality must be your prime concern in all areas likely to be seen and used by the public. Avoid, if you can, display units that cannot be moved. All display units should be easily shifted to meet the needs of the day.

Externally, a new shop front may be necessary, though if the window bed is not more than a foot above pavement level, the existing front may be suitable. Find out whether you have any display space outside the shop. This can be useful if you intend to operate a cash-and-carry trade and still very helpful if not, used for plants and possibly for clearing lines. Access for loading and unloading at front or rear is essential (and the absence of same in 'arcade' shops is a real headache for the florist). Where possible, rear access is preferable.

Always use professional advice when negotiating a lease. Clauses need to be examined by a qualified expert in such matters, and it is in your interests to consult such a person.

Equipping the shop

As a trained florist you will probably have very good ideas about the equipment you will need in your shop. Also, you may be already recognised as a trading florist by one or more of the sundries houses which supply the trade. If you are not you will need to bring evidence of your shop and your intention to trade before you will be allowed to open an account. In certain circumstances cash purchases may be allowed, but in order to make a wise choice of equipment you should visit at least two or three of the major sundries suppliers. If in doubt, always carry a copy of your letter-heading and your business card with you. In opening a new business these must be your first priority once the premises and opening date have been agreed.

Initially, do not buy more than your immediate requirements. It is easy to be carried away by 'unrepeatable offers' and special quantity prices. Make sure that the design and usefulness of any piece of equipment is right for your purposes before you buy in quantity. Avoid special offers brought to your door, or regard them with extreme caution. (A store-room full of wicker baskets worth £900 was once unloaded onto an unsuspecting newcomer to the trade.)

No doubt you know the things you will need, and the likely quantities, but the following list of reminders may be helpful:

Buckets and display vases   Metal, or of plastic materials. Various sizes.
Scissors and knives   Select for practical usage. Expensive knives get lost and the cheaper plastic handled variety is just as useful.
Wrapping paper, transparent wrapping   The choice is wide and a suppliers representative will call at your request.
Cards   Both greeting and for funeral tributes. Choose to suit your likely customers and, initially, not too many of any one design.
Display equipment   Adjustable units and shelf units. Always necessary but settle in before you spend too much upon these.
Staplers and/or pins,   Sellotape in a dispenser
Ribbons   Start with a wide range but not too much of any one colour. The paler shades are usually more popular.
Card envelopes   which can carry the name and address of the recipient.
Stub wires   A range to cover your immediate needs.
Frames   Plastic/foam, plus a few wire frames if preferred.
Mossing wire or string, wreathwrap, stem tape

Flower foam Several different foams are offered and you should experiment to find out which suits you the best.

No doubt you will think of other items. Remember that new florists' aids are constantly being introduced, and regular visits to a major sundries house can be very beneficial.

Staffing

In determining what your likely needs will be, it is necessary to take into account the size of the premises, the volume of business anticipated in the early stages, and the very nature of the business you intend to conduct.

Where one has the backing of family (husband/wife/son/daughter possibly) the early stages can be entirely a family affair. But to start alone, without any backing, is dangerous. Even in the most modest circumstances, in which it may seem prudent to limit severely display and services, a breaking point will be reached, and either the business will fail or there will be a break-down in health. In the following chapter the likely programme of work in an average florist's shop is outlined. It can be expanded or contracted according to the size of the business but it cannot be ignored.

Insurance

Your premises must be properly insured against the usual risks of fire, flood and theft, plus a third-party clause to cover customers and staff against accidents of any kind. It may be prudent also to arrange cover for cash-in-transit. Even when the bank is next door things can go wrong.

Legal notices

Retail shops are required by law to obtain and display notices relating to the employment of staff, their working hours, etc. Forms are usually available from local council offices. If you have not employed staff on a full-time basis before, it would be prudent to obtain the necessary legal guidance from the same offices, or from your local employment office.

Fire regulations   See Appendix page 148.

Daily operations in a flower shop

Maintenance of display is utterly important. Just as litter and untidiness will detract, tidiness and a sense of order will attract the eye. Indeed, some degree of tidying may be necessary after every customer, depending upon the nature of the purchase. A mop or cloth should be kept in a handy, but not too obvious, place. Windows and mirrors should be polished daily as a matter of routine. When not in use, buckets, vases and other containers should be stored clean and free of any debris. They should be rinsed in warm water, adding a cap-full of bleach to 4.5 litres of water. If a container is very stained, use hot water and allow the mixture to stand in the container for half an hour. Rinse thoroughly before storing upside down. Floors must be kept free of any litter which might cause you or your customer to slip or stumble. The van, or car used for deliveries, should be cleaned regularly and should be seen as a credit to the business.

All stock in trade must be inspected daily and serviced as required. The water in which cut-flowers are standing should be changed daily, unless you are using a recommended flower preservative such as *Chrysol*. This acts as a cleaning and feeding agent, and the daily change of water is not necessary. Water levels in the vases should be checked, however, and topped up where necessary. The stems of all flowers offered for sale should be clean and there should be no foliage actually in the water. A further check of both quantities and condition should be made each evening and/or before ordering further supplies.

Conditioning cut-flowers and plants

All flowers will require some 'conditioning' for sale, and the general procedures are as follows: (The specific needs of certain flowers are described in a later chapter, and under 'Servicing' on page 84).

Flowers should be unpacked from their boxes as soon as possible after arrival and stood in water. (The latter is not necessary for flowers arriving in aqua-packs, which are already in water.)

Stems should be trimmed, preferably with a sharp knife and about 25 mm removed from the ends. Scissors may be used if sharp, and certain stems – notably those of chrysanthemums and some carnations – may be persuaded to break cleanly and easily. Do not hammer stems; this does no good and only increases the amount of debris in a vase.

Remove all foliage which may be immersed in the water – other foliage should be allowed to remain attached. Deep water is not necessary, for flowers take in almost all their water supplies from the ends of the stems. The use of a flower preservative is recommended for all flowers taken into stock.

Use cool water (tap temperature) for all flowers unless recommended otherwise. (See also page 42).

Cool or cold storage is recommended for most flowers. If you use a cooler or cold-room equipment, follow the maker's instructions to the letter, unless and until you find some minor variations of temperature necessary. There is rarely any need to adjust. Long storage of flowers in a cooler is not recommended, and anything over three days can seriously shorten the vase life of the flowers once restored to normal conditions. Keep your cold-room very clean and tidy and remember that a cooler is not a grave-yard for unsaleable flowers.

A well-ventilated cellar may relieve you of the need to buy a cooler and if this facility exists beneath your shop it can be of immense value.

As with cut flowers, plants should be released from their packing as soon as possible after arrival and checked for quantity, condition and immediate needs such as water (many plants travel relatively dry and once out in the air will suffer if not watered). However, water with care. There should be a daily routine to check all plants for possible needs, but water should only be applied where necessary. Over-watering can be very dangerous. Plants should be inspected and cleaned every other day, removing any blooms that have wilted and any unsightly foliage.

All deliveries of stock should be checked carefully to ensure that grade, quantity and condition are as invoiced (or as seen if it is a market purchase). Complaints registered immediately are usually honoured – those made later can be in dispute.

Rubbish should never be retained within the shop or workroom overnight. Decaying plant material will give off a gas which is detrimental to living flowers, and a sack of debris can be a killer. If it is not possible to have it removed daily, store it outside. Ventilation in the shop is necessary but draughts can be dangerous. Use reasonable discretion in relation to outside weather conditions and remember that extremes of heat, humidity and frost are all damaging to your stock.

Tools should be kept clean and sharp. Where several persons are employed about the shop it is advisable that they be provided with their individual tools, for if there is a general tool-box, nobody seems to care.

Orders for floristry or simply for gifts should be filed immediately they are taken, and experience has shown that a series of compartments upon a wall, with clip-boards hanging within, each having the orders for a specific day of the week clipped to it, is the most practicable method. The compartments should be marked clearly from Monday to Saturday, and a further compartment labelled 'next week' will avoid confusion over advance orders. The day and date of the order should be clearly shown at the bottom of each sheet. (Alternative systems may need this to appear at the top. What is important is the convenience and ease of access to each day's orders.) As a daily drill, the orders for tomorrow should be checked for both volume and supplies needed and, of course, the 'next week' file should be included in this essential scan of work to be done.

Buying

Whenever possible handle produce of the highest obtainable quality, which means, in simple terms, flowers that will give immediate satisfaction and reasonable vase-life in average conditions.

Grading of flowers, and a coding relating to stem length, is applied by the grower and is accepted as a scale of standard by the trade generally. Condition, however, may vary considerably throughout the grades, and it is by no means unusual for the lower grading (shorter stemmed) to have as good, if not better flower heads than those in the top grades. This applies particularly to roses at certain seasons of the year. So you must be your own judge and your own assessor of quality. In general, firmness/crispness of the flower heads carried upon strong clean stems and with full-toned clean foliage, these are the first prime tests which you must apply. Experience will soon take over and you will see very quickly what is meant by an 'instinct' for assessment.

Because flowers are subject to seasonal conditions, there are no firm rules, and these suggestions must be taken as a guide, or as a point of reference when in doubt.

(Further details on buying will be found in Part 4 pages 127 to 132.)

Buying at or through a market is better than buying from the mobile wholesaler at your door. But few of us have time to attend markets regularly, and in many cases the florist is dependent upon the supplies brought to him, or perhaps sent from a 'country order' wholesaler in Covent Garden. Those coming into the trade will be wise to keep their options open and not settle for one or another system without some experimental purchases. It is wise, too, to visit a market occasionally and see the whole picture for yourself. The main objective must be to obtain, at the most reasonable price, goods of the quality you require. The best of wholesalers will have an occasional failure, and the worst will have an occasional success – it is the service over a period that matters most to the florist.

Flower relay

Once your shop is fully established you may well wish to extend into flower relay business. Possibly your customers will begin to ask for the service.

There are two organisations which, through their members, engage in flower relay, and they are:

Interflora British Unit Ltd, Interflora House, Sleaford, Lincolnshire
and
British Teleflower Service Ltd, 146 Bournemouth Road, Chandler's Ford, Eastleigh, Hampshire.

An enquiry to the headquarters of either will bring you information upon the terms and conditions of membership. However, you must not expect that either will be willing to accept you as a member without a detailed inspection of your premises and evidence of your qualifications as a florist. To avoid unnecessary disappointment, you would be wise to compare your shop and standards of service with those of other florists in your area who are engaged in flower relay. You will be expected at least to measure up to local standards.

PART TWO

The year round

Many flowers, once regarded as seasonal, are now available for most, if not all, of the year. These comprise the first list which follows. The quality and range of colours may vary a little, and your supplier will advise you upon market conditions. Nevertheless, as retailer and supplier to the general public you have a duty to make *your* needs known.

Alstroemeria Alstroemeria is usually at its best in spring and early summer, but is available in good quality, though in a less wide range of colours, at all other times. It has a long vase life and many attributes of the perfect florists' flower. It is adaptable, useful in make-up work and delightful in decorations. Usually it is marketed in wraps of ten or occasionally five sprays, with many flower heads per stem, several open and the rest in advanced bud stage. Most of these will open in the right conditions. Stems should be trimmed before placing in water, removing any foliage which might become immersed in water. Use a recommended flower preservative in the water which should not be more than 10 to 12 cm deep. Change and/or inspect water daily as the stems are soft and will disintegrate quickly if bacteria gets in. The outdoor alstroemeria, known as the 'Lily of Peru', has a seasonal popularity, usually in July and August.

Carnations Single headed carnations, sometimes called 'standards' have been a popular year-round flower for many years. They are still much in demand for weddings, as buttonholes, in decoration work and as gifts. Carnation growing in Britain has decreased sharply in the last twenty years and most of our supplies now come from abroad, usually packed in wraps containing twenty or twenty-five. Overall their quality is superb and modern treatment after harvesting can ensure a very long life for a quality carnation – up to three weeks is claimed for some specified sendings. In buying carnations look for firm, crisp flowers, on strong stems of deep dusty green colouring. Break, or cut a small piece from the ends before placing in water. The flower will take up water more easily if this break is between the 'nodes' (or joints which occur in the stems). The flowers enjoy a well ventilated position with good light but they do not require direct sunshine. Avoid buying those with split calyxes as these will develop into lop-sided flowers. Never store carnations in close vicinity with fruit, and carefully remove any faded flowers from a vase as soon as they are noticed. Fading is usually indicated by a softening of the petals and a tendency to curl inwards. If in doubt, separate from the remainder of your stock as such flowers can damage others by emitting ethylene gas – the dying carnation is a menace to all others around it.

Spray carnations Spray carnations are generally bunched and wrapped in fives or tens, and each 'spray' may consist of several strong flowers and advanced buds held on dainty stems. Treatment is the same as for the standard carnations, though a vase life of more than a week is unusual. There is a wide range of colours for most of the year, though overall quality will vary from season to season.

Chrysanthemums Most of the chrysanthemums sold today are of the spray or 'all-year-round' varieties. There are wide variation in colour, form and general habit. Good quality spray can have a vase life of up to two weeks. It is tough, durable and will lend itself to every aspect of a florist's work. Poor quality spray is trouble and can only be used for massed basing.

Spray is marketed in wraps containing five, ten, fifteen or even twenty stems per wrap. Best quality is usually found in the fives or tens, though some English growers still pack larger quantities regardless of quality. Thus it is wise to be careful in buying. Flower heads should be firm and in most varieties showing a green centre. Stems should be clean, green and strong. If the pack is floppy, it is suspect, for if it flops as a pack, how much more floppy will the single stems be.

Stems that are stripped and brown at the ends indicate a long, perhaps too long a period of conditioning after harvesting – avoid such if you can. It is recognised that the flowers are difficult to assess in those varieties that have no green centre. However, to the touch they should feel firm, if not actually crisp. If they feel damp, or wet, or show any brown petals they should be avoided for if the condition is obvious whilst packed, there is sure to be more trouble within.

However, there will be those occasions when you are seeking good flower-heads for massing and will not be too worried about their stems. Experience will come to your rescue and your order sheets will be your guide.

Chrysanthemums should be treated as for all main-line flowers. Use a suitable flower preservative, and stand in 12 to 15 cm of water after trimming the ends of the stems with a knife, or sometimes a clean break will suffice. Remove any foliage that will be immersed in water but DO NOT strip the stems of all their foliage – it is not necessary and disfigures the flowers for eventual sale. (Who wants a flower on top of a walking stick?) If your chrysanthemums arrive looking unduly limp, use warm water to encourage a quick recovery (temperature should not be above blood heat).

The single flowering varieties are particularly interesting. Generally they are daisy-shaped and come in delightful shades of pink, mauve, orange and red. You may have to badger your wholesaler for these, but make sure that you get what you want, and not what he thinks you should have.

Chrysanthemum 'standards' or 'blooms' are often packed in boxes to avoid damage, and many of these come from English growers. They are at their best in the autumn, though limited supplies are available throughout the summer. Blooms should be clean, and intact: those in wraps are liable to have some damage, so buy with care. Avoid any with soft and twisted stems. A standard should be able to support the weight of the bloom without drooping dismally over the side of the vase. Look for flowers with greenish centres. Avoid those showing dampness and remember that loose petals in the box, or wrap, mean damaged blooms. Treatment on arrival is the same as for spray chrysanthemums, but do not crowd too many into one vase as damage will occur when the heads rub together. Naturally grown blooms sometimes have very hard and woody stems, and you may be tempted to use a hammer – but don't, for a cut and perhaps a split to open the stem is all that is needed. When using blooms for an order, pack with great care, especially with the incurved varieties which are easily damaged by a careless knock.

Freesia   Freesia, once thought of only as a spring flower, is now with us for most of the year. However, it is at its best during winter and spring and even into early summer, whilst for the rest of the year it is somewhat less reliable. Consult your wholesaler if you are booking orders for any specific colours.

Buy freesia with one or two flowers on each stem and a strong line of buds to follow. The stems should be strong, of reasonable length and deep green in colour. Usually freesias are bunched in fives. Trim by removing a tiny piece of the stem only and place in cool water. Give the flowers space in which to develop without damaging each other, and use a flower preservative in the water.

The sleeves, in which many bunches of freesias are marketed, should be removed for shop sales, and only left on if the flowers are to be sold in the open air.

Gerbera   Once a rarety, the gerbera is with us for most of the year in dazzling colours. Great daisy-shaped flowers, held on thickish stems, they are particularly useful in decorative arrangements and for display. They have one inbuilt problem – they do not take water easily and, if unsupported tend to bend and bow their heads in any unlikely direction. The trouble is reduced if they are put into warm water with flower preservative upon arrival. Trim the stems first, of course, and put them fairly closely together in a tall, straight-sided vase or bucket. A few hours in a darkish place, free from draught, will usually do the trick. Some florists thread a supporting wire through the hollow centre of the stem, but this gives an artificial look to the flower.

Never buy buddy-looking or immature flowers as these rarely can be persuaded to drink. Look for fully formed flowers, in full colour, and if there is a hole in the very centre of the 'daisy', it is a good sign.

One grower still markets his gerbera in trays of twelve or fifteen, and with the heads threaded through holes so that the tray can be hung above a bucket with the stems reaching down into the water, the theory being that this will help the stems to become straight and once straight and full of water there will be no more trouble. It is worth trying if such packs come your way. Generally, gerberas take longer to condition than most flowers, and some will take as long as two/three days to straighten up.

Gladioli The gladioli are with us throughout the year, because once the natural season is over in England there are imports available from all over Europe. They grow from corms, have heavy stems and sword-like foliage, and one stem can carry many flowers and buds. Rarely, however, do the top buds open and most of the beauty of gladioli is in the first three or four flowers. They arrive bunched, usually in tens, but are most often sold by the stem. As with many other bulb or corm flowers, they can stand for a day without water, and can even be sold dry as long as they are placed into a bucket that will hold them in an upright position. Ideally, however, gladioli should be unpacked and stood in water as soon as they arrive, for the longer they are left in a horizontal position, the more twisted will the bud stems become. Where they are extremely long and twisted it is often advisable to trim the top, leaving perhaps a likely three or four to open above the actual flowers. Do not leave an obvious stump of stem showing, however. Take about 12 mm off the stems before placing into water, and remove any foliage that is not actually attached to the stem. In buying, look carefully at the flowers that are open and at the buds, and reject any showing discolouration due to dampness, or any that are actually wet. Our weather is not always kind to gladioli growers, but you have to think of your customers and of the disappointment that can be caused when seemingly good looking flowers open blotched and transparent. Remove any faded flowers as they occur, carefully pulling the whole flower out of the calyx without damage. This will encourage the buds to open, and such stems can still be most useful in decoration and designing. Also, perhaps, for a weekend display. The *gladioli primulinus* varieties, available in spring and summer, require the same treatment as detailed above. They are especially useful in lighter decoration work and in wedding floristry.

Iris Blue and mauve irises are with us for most of the year, but the yellow and white varieties are not always obtainable. It is wise to consult your supplier before booking a firm order.

Stems and foliage should be clean and crisp to the touch. Flowers should be showing colour, preferably with the tips of the petals breaking from the calyx, or even in a half-open condition. The flowers should be dry – any suspicion of water or dampness will mean that the flowers will open showing small brown spots which entirely disfigure the flower. If you are offered buds, with no colour showing, it may mean that the flowers have been harvested too early, and the eventual flowers may be of poor quality. Limpness of stem is not of necessity a sign of poor quality and may be observed in batches giving high quality bloom. Yellowing ends or shrivelling may indicate too long a sojourn in cold store. Upon arrival trim the stems removing about 12 mm in most cases, but rather more when the stem ends are white. This section should be removed entirely. Use cold water, or luke-warm water if you need the flowers to open quickly. Do not allow steam around the buds. Deep water is not necessary; about 10 cm is sufficient.

Lilies Many beautiful varieties of lily are available today, and for most of the year. The quality and range of colours may vary from season to season and the peak is reached in late spring and summer. Lilies are most useful for both decoration and make-up, and they have a long vase life. Generally they are marketed in bud with perhaps one or two flowers open on each stem. Many of the tighter buds will open eventually in reasonable conditions and the use of a preservative and food in the water is recommended. As with most bulb flowers, the stems tend to be soft and vulnerable to bacteria, so remove any leaves that may be immersed in water and trim the ends of the stems very cleanly with a sharp knife. Deep water is not necessary. Consult your wholesaler upon varieties and colours available at any particular time. *Lilium longiflorum*, or *Henryii* is the white, long-trumpeted lily used in large decorative work, in churches and for funeral work. The treatment is as described above, but fewer buds are carried on each head and development is slower. The Arum Lily (*Zantedeschia aethiopica*) is seasonal being available from January to May in most years. Its heavy fleshy stems can be straightened by gently pulling them through the hand – water is essential to keep the growth healthy, and it will be found that most Arums are marketed in half-open stage. Avoid the fully open as they do not travel well and frequently show bruising on the great waxy petal. A useful lily for formal decoration, and preferring coolish conditions.

Roses The rose is the flower for so many occasions and particularly desirable for the sentimental and celebratory occasions of this life. Hence its popularity. But it is not the easiest of flowers for the florist to handle. Whilst far from fragile, it has a relatively short vase life, and once fully open the bloom has little commercial value. Home grown and Channel Island grown roses are more predictable than the imported, because all too often the latter are stored in a cooler for too long before being marketed. Results may satisfy for an occasion but their vase life is very unsatisfactory. So buy with care: not too forward (open) and not too tight (very buddy). Those required for sale or for same day orders will need water, at once, before being sent out. If the stems seem limp, warm water is permissible in order to give them a good start. First, however, trim the ends of the stems and remove foliage that might become immersed. Those offered for sale, or sent out as cut-flowers should be de-thorned – a prickly and tedious job but necessary in a quality business. (The use of a sharp knife is recommended rather than laborious snipping with scissors. There are some de-thorning gadgets on the market but none is recommended as they tend to destroy both thorns *and* foliage.)

Some roses develop slowly, others open very quickly. The weather will accelerate the process, and sudden hot weather can cause real troubles for the florist. Should roses seem already too advanced upon delivery, they should be left standing without water for a few more hours. This will at least delay the rapid opening which could occur when they are placed in water. The problem is not so acute if you have a cooler.

Roses that are limp and seem not to be able to take up water may be given the short hot-water treatment in a bucket containing about 10 cm of water, not quite boiling. Allow the roses ten to fifteen minutes standing in this, then return them to luke-warm water. Another method of restoring crispness to the stems is to immerse the whole stem and flower head in cool water for an hour or so. Failure to drink is sometimes due to air-locks in the tiny capillary tubes which carry water up to the head.

Quality roses can be recognised by firm, clean flower-heads, strong stems and foliage of good colour. Damp spots on the petals can indicate trouble throughout the flower, and weak, yellowish stems just below the flower head indicate a rose that will never take up water again. (Undue heat just before the rose was harvested is usually the cause of the latter.) Always use a flower preservative in the water, as roses like to grow.

Miniature roses are often in demand for wedding work. They should be treated as above but generally give very little trouble, and tend to develop slowly. If bought fully open they will usually stand for several days.

Seasonal flowers

SPRING

Daffodils and narcissi   Most daffodils and narcissi are marketed in relatively buddy condition. For most varieties of daffodil the 'goose-neck' stage of the bud is ideal for the florist. 'Goose-neck' means that the bud has turned at right-angles to the stem and has begun to burst, showing the petal colouring at the extreme end. Be cautious if you are offered daffodils with pencil-straight stems and buds, for these may be in too-backward a condition, liable to open slowly and give flowers of poor quality. Some varieties react better than others and the short trumpeted hybrids generally survive without much damage. Over-long periods in cold-storage are damaging. Flowers or buds stored for more than two or three days begin to deteriorate, and with the bud daffodil, a long period in the cold may cause flower development to cease entirely. So, when buying, avoid those boxes of buds that show advanced shrivelling at the ends of the stems. Some drying out is to be expected, but more than 25 mm of wasted stem is an indicator of a long period of time since harvesting. A further danger signal is yellowing of the outer tissue surrounding the buds, accompanied by limpness of the stems – such buds will not give satisfaction, however well they are treated after you have bought them.

Assuming, however, that you have bought good quality daffodils in goose-neck condition, they should be trimmed to open the stems and stood in cold water. A flower preservative is not essential, but it is wise to change the water after a few hours, to remove the gummy fluid which exudes from the stems. (This, by the way, is dangerous to other flowers, and all daffodils should be treated in this way before being used in a mixed arrangement.)

If you want to hold your daffodils back for a day or so, they may be left standing in dry buckets for at least a day. The cooler will help to retard them, too, but remember that three days is the absolute limit. Towards the end of the season it may be impossible to locate daffodils in bud and you may be offered those fully open. Look into the flower and if the stamens are covered in pollen, that flower will be dying within 24 hours. If the stamens are clean and greenish, then the flower has a reasonable two to three days vase life left. At this end of the season daffodils are not expensive usually, and are taken into stock for quick sales. A thinning or 'papery' look to the outer petals will indicate a rapid collapse of the flower.

Most of the above applies equally to narcissi, although the multi-headed varieties are usually marketed with one or two flowers already open. Nevertheless, these flowers should be crisp to the touch, clean and dry.

Tulips Tulips should be bought in bud, but not at the 'all-green' stage where there is no evidence of the eventual colour of the bloom. Ideally, the colour should be seen flooding into the green petals. Foliage should be crisp and green and although some varieties have long leaves, these should not extend far above the flower heads. The stems should be sturdy and well able to support the flower. Those that are limp and unduly slender just below the flower-head will probably give trouble in taking in water and may remain floppy in spite of all your care. Healthy tulips may have their stems straightened by their being wrapped firmly in paper and stood in water in semi-darkness for a few hours. Stems should be trimmed as for other spring flowers and water need not be deep, 10 cm is sufficient. If yellowish foliage is observed, it can mean that the tulips have been too long in cold storage. Also, when buying, be alert for any evidence of 'spot', which is a virus that infects some varieties. It is not easy to detect in its early stages, but to be safe you should reject any that show a light pimply rash upon leaves or buds. The pimples soon turn to brown spots, especially in mild and damp conditions, rendering the flowers unfit for sale.

There is a wide range of colours available, and considerable variations in stem-length and habit. Quality, however, tends to fall off towards the end of the season, and the field-grown tulips are not usually worth handling.

Hyacinths Hyacinths are most often handled as pot plants with the flowers growing on the bulbs. You may require them for wedding work, however, and bunched in threes or fives they may be purchased well ahead of requirement. Stand them in water and store in a cooler or some well ventilated place.

Anemones Anemones may be bought at most seasons of the year as many are grown abroad. However, their traditional 'season' is from late autumn to May. They should be purchased as fully developed flowers, cup-shaped and showing full colour and on strong stems. Avoid those which are offered in green-bud stage as they rarely develop into satisfactory flowers. A mass of green foliage surrounding the flower is not necessarily good, and more often accompanies undersized, poor quality flowers. Be alert also for damping or condensation upon flowers or foliage, as brown spots are likely to appear within a few hours.

Violets Violets often need to be plunged into cold water for a few minutes upon arrival. Shaken out, they may still be sold from the box afterwards, and will look all the better for their dip. To be attractive, violets must appear crisp.

SUMMER

For many florists, summer brings the possibility of handling many herbaceous and annual flowers that are grown in Britain, as well as some of the rarer items that come from overseas. Some are only available for a short week or so whilst others, like the delphinium, may be found for most of the summer.

They all need attention which is not dissimilar to that which is advised for year-round flowers. Stems must be trimmed, excess foliage removed and they should be stood in water as soon as possible after delivery. Those stood out in the sunshine will die much more quickly than those kept in cool shady conditions. Use a flower preservative in the water and, in the case of stocks and several other of the herbacious group, water must be changed daily if you are to avoid unpleasant smells.

Weather will control supplies. Some seasons will bring a wealth of annuals in good hard condition whilst another season, perhaps a hot sunny June, will reduce our annual supplies to a trickle. Unduly wet and cold weather will ruin some crops entirely.

Currently there is a trend back towards the natural flowers of summer and the wise florist will observe this trend and use it to advantage. The following is a short list of good selling lines. It is not complete and from experience you will be able to add other items. The important thing is to keep an open mind.

Asters Double and single varieties are available in late summer, and as the popular Michaelmas daisy in autumn.

Campanula Several species of herbaceous campanula are very useful in decoration work. Mostly blue or white. Also useful is the biennial Canterbury Bell, in a variety of colours.

Chrysanthemum maximum Many varieties, mostly white and ranging from the large dog daisy to the double Esther Reid, Horace Reid and Wirral Pride.

Aquilegia   Long-spurred columbine. This is not an easy flower to handle but decorative. It comes in several colours and has only a short vase life.

Achillia   Great golden-yellow heads. It is very useful in large decoration work but not attractive as a cut flower.

Delphinium   Immensely useful in decoration and for display work but not generally reckoned for day-to-day sales. It needs plenty of water. Some folk even try filling the stems with water before placing into a vase but the effectiveness of this is not proven. Larger varieties tend to drop petals after first day. Smaller varieties (eg Blue Fountains and similar strains) are better for make-up and will not drop petals so early. Colours include all shades of blue and mauve, also white.

Doronicum   An early summer flower. It is golden yellow, very striking and can fill a gap in the cut-flower supplies after the daffodils have gone. Not particularly useful in make up.

Gypsophila   Annual gypsophila is still available in some areas. It consists of little white bells on very soft stems. But the popular 'gyp' today is the variety once called Bristol Fairy, now grown in profusion abroad and arriving in quality and quantity unheard of in previous years. It is with us for most of the year. It is popular for make-up, decorative work and frequently requested as a back-up to gift flowers. It requires only that it be stood in water with a flower preservative which will keep it alive and growing for at least two weeks. Never allow it to dry out, however, because the tiny florets will shrivel beyond recovery.

Honesty   This is usually marketed dry, or nearly so because its attraction is in the silvery-white disc that holds the seed. If the stems are still green it can be dried off very easily by hanging, or standing it in a cool well-ventilated shed. It can also be dyed in any colour to suit taste but this is not recommended.

Lupin This attractive border flower is useful only for immediate decoration work. Available in shades of pink, blue, mauve and orange, it is nevertheless a menace because it starts to drop its lower flowers almost as soon as it is stood in water. Use with care and prepare for much tidying up.

Paeony One of the earliest and possibly the most useful of herbaceous flowers. It appears usually in mid-May and is available for about a month. Huge buds (buy in bud stage if you can) looking like the heads of drumsticks open into great cup-shaped flowers, the most popular colours being pink and white. There are other varieties, however, smaller flowered and very attractive and if you are offered any they are well worth a trial. Because of its robust nature, the paeony is useful in all forms of decoration and display work. Never a dainty flower but an attractive back-up for May–June display.

Pinks Pinks and border carnations have a firm place in the summer sales pattern. There are many varieties, several of which are useful in massing funeral tributes. But the main appeal is as a cut flower, because the perfume and colours are delightful. Buy in small quantities, as they have a relatively short life.

Pyrethrum An old-fashioned and popular quick selling flower. It grows easily and cheaply and can never command a high price. The colours are garish, pink and red mostly, and the shape is of the common daisy. However, the Pyrethrum should not be ignored and with the return of many garden flowers to fashion, it could well be carried along with the tide.

Sea Lavender This is a form of statice which can be dried and used for massing the bases of funeral designs. If you buy it green, commence drying whilst the little mauve florets are still open – in this way they will retain their colour, even when dry. Bunches may be hung for drying, preferably in a well ventilated shed. Another statice, **Incana**, may be treated in the same way if you are able to obtain it. It dries into a stiff, brittle bundle of stems, grey in colour. If intended for massing, it can be wired into units whilst green, and assembled for massing after it has dried.

Scabious This is available in mid-summer for a period of several weeks. Usual variety is Clive Greaves – or similar more recent introductions. Colour is light mauve. It is a dainty though by no means a small flower. Vase life is two to three days in average temperature. If the centre is fluffy, it is already over the top and will drop within twelve hours. Buy always when centres are firm and green and petals still not quite uncurled. A useful flower in make-up.

The annual scabious (pin-cushion flower) is rarely marketed now. If seen it is useful for quick sales and table decoration work. Usually multi-coloured in one bunch, eg pink, white and mauve.

Solomon's Seal This consists of long curving branches holding elongated bell-like florets of white. Useful in decoration work – invaluable some would say – but not likely to be a quick seller.

Sweet William A biennial of the dianthus family, Sweet William has a firm place in the hearts of most florists. The wide range of colouring, the adaptability of the clusters of wide-eyed florets and its attractiveness in display, all make for its popularity. Sadly it has only a short season, usually early June to mid-July but well worth its place. It will stand in water for several days without wilting provided it is kept cool.

Stocks Column stocks are available in early summer and make a welcome addition to one's display. Sweetly scented, they are useful in every aspect of a florist's work. One word of caution – stems disintegrate very quickly and foul-smelling water can be a problem in a few hours. Use a good preservative, or add a capful of bleach to about 4 to 5 litres of water.

The latter will keep the water clean and does no harm to the flowers.

Sweet peas Sweet peas can claim top scores for perfume, and for a wide range of delightful pastel colours. Well grown and on long strong stems they have at best about a three-day vase life. Very useful for June weddings and for gift flowers, but the season is short for top quality, and once into July cannot be relied upon. Almost all those arriving in our markets are home-grown. A small-grower or even an amateur may have to be your sources of supply.

Marigolds Marigolds are returning to popularity as a cut flower. Three varieties are of interest; the calendula (large, flattish double flowers) the African (large knob-shaped heads of yellow and orange on strong stems), and the several varieties of French marigold – some all gold or all yellow, and others splashed liberally with rich brown. The latter are the easiest to handle and have a particular appeal to those seeking bright but small flowers. Marigolds will have little use in make-up work, unless specially requested by a customer, but should be offered experimentally as a cash and carry cut flower.

Zinnias These brilliantly coloured annuals come late in the summer and appeal to all who enjoy drama. Their vase life is not long but they are most useful in decoration work where colour is needed. The minature or Liliput zinnias are most attractive, too, and are yet another example of the garden flowers which are becoming more popular. All are offered usually in mixed coloured bunches. Avoid any that seem damp or have water in and among the blooms as they will 'spot' easily.

Liatris The liatris is a summer season flower as grown in Britain but can be obtained from abroad at most other seasons of the year. Its rosy-purple spikes are most useful in all decoration work and it has a long vase life. Cool storage is not recommended, however, and in buying you should look for spikes that are already well furnished with open florets.

AUTUMN
Besides bringing in a crop of naturally-grown chrysanthemums, and some late gladioli, the autumn is a harvest time for foliages, both deciduous such as the beech and chestnut, and evergreens of all varieties. Not all of these reach our markets as they should, and if

situated in provincial or semi-rural area the florist is wise to seek local suppliers.

Dahlias These flowers come into their own late in August and, given reasonable weather, are with us for most of September. Like zinnias, much of their charm is in their multiplicity of colours. Size and shape vary widely, but most useful and popular are 'small decorative' types and the smaller pompons. Generally, dahlias travel badly and need to be trimmed and stood in water as soon as possible after arrival. Their foliage is plentious and usually untidy and should be reduced by the removal of all from the lower stems and a proportion of that which may surround the flowers. Dahlias have about three days of vase life in normal conditions. In buying never accept any that have moisture in the blooms as these will collapse quickly, buy in small batches little and often, whilst the season lasts.

Statice *Limonium*, or coloured statice, may be purchased dried at any time of the year, but it arrives fresh and green in autumn. The florist has the choice of selling it, using it, or drying it for future use. Mostly it is used for massing upon funeral tributes, though it has some attraction as part of a dried arrangement. Upon arrival it does not need to be stood in water. The stems are liable to disintegrate even in the best of conditions, and selling from a dry bucket or box is recommended. Drying can take place as for other varieties of statice, but wiring for future use whilst green is not recommended as there is considerable shrinkage in the tissue as it dries out and the units easily fall apart when handled. Statice is never a number one selling item, but it is part of the florist's scene.

Throughout the year, there are several other types of flower that a florist may be required to handle, such as Lily of the Valley, Eremurus gentian, myosotis, stephanotis, orchids of various kinds, antirrhinum and agapanthus. No doubt there are others but none is likely to be a regular stock item in the early stages of a new business. However, if in doubt, here are some basic rules:
Avoid extremes of heat or cold (above 24°C and below 3.3°C).

Allow the flowers to take water as required.
Avoid direct sunshine and draughts.
Cover the flowers with tissue paper if a draught is unavoidable.
Gentle overhead spraying with clear water is beneficial in hot or dry conditions but DO NOT DRENCH.
Use a recommended flower food and preservative in the water.

CHRISTMAS FOLIAGES (holly, mistletoe and Christmas trees) All of these items require space far above their earning capacity. But if you have space to spare (preferably outside) and a tolerant staff, there could be some return and some sales to people who might not have come to you otherwise.

Christmas trees are the worst of all the space gobblers. They also become time-gobblers, for many customers like to go through the whole of your stock in order to find the one with the right shape. If you decide to stock them, sell out before the last few days. Never re-stock for late sales because there are none.

Holly, in bulk or bunched, is another greedy item. It is difficult to handle at the best of times and earns very small rewards. It has one virtue – it makes the shop look Christmassy, and it can be sold right up to the last few minutes of Christmas Eve.

Mistletoe has a quaint but declining popularity; perhaps its traditional purpose has been whittled away in a permissive age. Buy in just enough to keep your regulars happy. No more.

Holly wreaths for memorial use have lost much of their popularity in city areas. There are many reasons for this: cremation and less cemetary visiting among them, also the quite appalling lack of quality, workmanship, and utter bad taste in the plastic flowers so often stuck around them. Perhaps because they are so unpleasant to handle, they have been avoided by florists and I cannot blame them.

The small door-wreath, or holly ring, is another matter. It is coming back into fashion as a welcoming message for all callers and, for those who prefer sophistication, as a Christmas decoration. It can be made of holly, cones, berries and any suitable dried materials – even nuts!

Advent, celebrated seriously in Germany, is often overlooked in this country. The Advent wreath, however, is a charming and very acceptable decoration. Generally it is made of foliage, with cones and berries and with four candles, symbolising the four weeks to Christmas. You may well be asked to make one or show one in your window. It will attract attention or, at least, questions.

Plant care

Indoor plants have become a very significant sales item for many florists. The extent to which they can be handled depends mostly upon space available and the only exceptions occur where the premises are very small, or are part of a large and departmentalised garden centre. Detailed advice upon plant care is included on pages 88 to 93, but following are some general rules concerning their care whilst carried in stock:

On arrival

Check carefully for shortages, damage in transit, disturbance from their pots and correctness of specification (are they what you ordered?) Some plants travel dry and will need careful watering as soon as possible – others may be damp and quite happy. To be sure, check carefully using the tips of the fingers upon the soil as a guide. If soil is moist or even damp no water is needed for the time being.

Used in display, or in storage, plants need protection from daughts and extremes of temperature. Packaging should be removed from all except very delicate subjects such as the African violets which are better displayed in their box which is usually screened. Plants which are wrapped individually should have that wrap removed, particularly if it is of soft clinging cellophane, which tends to cut off the air from the foliage.

Display

Outside display is very vulnerable, particularly from sunshine and wind. Frost, too, is a killer. It is suggested that your display, whether inside or outside the shop, should be *above* floor level so as to avoid casual damage from passers-by. Plants displayed as a group are more likely to be noticed than those which are scattered amongst the cut-flower display. Nevertheless, large foliage plants can be used most effectively as a backing for cut flowers.

Do not overcrowd your plant display. You may have a special display unit as part of your shop fitting, but if it is overcrowded it loses its effectiveness. Label all plants with their name and price, and arrange for basic care card or leaflet to go with every plant. Some plants carry a care label – make sure that this is appropriate and sufficient.

In-store care

Water should be applied as needed and not as a daily routine. Very few plants indeed require water daily and over-watering will produce all sorts of trouble for you – and losses. However, two plants which may require help daily are the azalea and (in season) the hydrangea. Neither should be allowed to dry out, for whilst the hydrangea can sometimes be revived by immersion in a bucket of water, the azalea will not recover.

A short list of some of the more popular indoor plants is given on page 54. There are many others, particularly foliage plants, which are available in varying sizes for most of the year.

The so-called 'poisonous' plants

Anyone who is subject to skin allergy or asthma should be cautious and remain alert to the risks, however small they may be, in handling plant material. However, newspaper articles sometimes give the impression that every other plant sits waiting, triffid-like, to pounce upon the unsuspecting human being. Such is not the case, and it cannot be said loudly enough that almost all of the current range of indoor plants are blameless and have no cannibalistic tendencies.

Anyone with hyper-sensitivity may find irritation following contact with the *primula obconica*, and possibly also from the stems of alstroemeria. It should be remembered, too, that occasionally quite

THE YEAR ROUND

This easy chart shows when plants are available ● and when they are 'best buys' ●

	Jan	Feb	Mar	Apr	May	Jun	Jul	Aug	Sep	Oct	Nov	Dec
Aphelandra (Zebra Plant)					●	●	●	●				
Azalea Indica	●	●	●							●	●	●
Begonia		●	●	●	●	●	●	●	●	●		
Calceolaria		●	●	●	●							
Chrysanthemum	●	●	●	●	●	●	●	●	●	●	●	●
Cineraria	●	●	●	●	●							
Cyclamen	●	●					●	●	●	●	●	●
Exacum					●	●	●	●				
Gloxinia					●	●	●	●				
Heather (Cape Erica)	●	●	●							●	●	●
Hydrangea			●	●	●	●						
Kalanchoe	●	●	●	●	●	●	●	●	●	●	●	●
Pelargonium				●	●	●	●					
Poinsettia	●								●	●	●	●
Polyanthus	●	●	●									
Primula Malacoides	●	●	●	●								
Saintpaulia (African Violet)	●	●	●	●	●	●	●	●	●	●	●	●
Schlumbergera (Easter Cactus)		●	●	●								
Solanum (Winter Cherry)										●	●	●
Zygocactus (Christmas Cactus)											●	●

serious skin problems can arise amongst those who handle the dry bulbs of hyacinths and narcissi. Casual handling, as perhaps by a customer, is unlikely to have any effect.

Two plants must be mentioned as carrying a potential threat, but only if you have a preference for chewing vile tasting leaves and berries. They are the solanum (Christmas Cherry) whose fruits have been known to attract children, and our old friend the dieffenbachia (or Dumb Cane). The effects are uncomfortable rather than fatal, but if you have any reason to suspect that a child has been so misguided, you should consult a doctor at once. The solanum is a member of the huge family of plants which include the tomato, potato, capsicum and deadly-nightshade, so, outside the home, the same precautions should be issued to any child: 'Eat nothing, unless you have first shown it to me!'

The dieffenbachia earns its strange common name from its sap, which, taken through the mouth can cause irritation and loss of voice. Temporarily, may I add, but uncomfortable, and if in doubt you should always consult a doctor. But do not blame your dieffenbachia every time you have a sore throat, as the chances of being affected in handling are very small indeed, especially if you follow the advice: NOW, WASH YOUR HANDS.

A few other plants bearing both berries and leaves that should never be eaten are:

Acuba (spotted laurel) berries and leaves
Laurel of any other kind
Euphorbia   any variety
Marantha
Berries from honeysuckle or ivy
Laburnum seeds.

An American florist, dealing with a public who seem to worry much more about their health than we do, has this notice in his shop:

'We would remind our clients that all plants sold by the florist are for decorative purposes, and are not a food source. Any plant material taken into the mouth by accident or in mischief, should be expelled immediately.'

Can't say fairer than that, can we?

Bulbs and dish gardens

Spring-flowering bulbs may be grown in pots and bowls, and from December through to April they are attractive additions to the above list. Daffodils, narcissi and hyacinths are particularly suitable, also some of the shorter early-flowering tulips. All of these should be purchased in backward condition as many customers prefer them that way.

Planted bowls, or 'dish-gardens' as they are sometimes called, are popular as presents, especially at Christmas time. They may be purchased ready planted, or you may prefer to plant your own, using plants from stock. If so, remember to place some pebbles and charcoal lumps in the bottom of the bowl, and after planting, water with care, and *only when needed*. Surplus water may be drained off by tipping the bowl in a corner of the sink. Choose your plants with care, and do not try to mix succulants (those which require little water) with the more thirsty plants such as azaleas, and most ferns. Plants with similar needs should be selected, and will give longer satisfaction in the home.

Diversification

Much has been written about the wider range of goods which can be sold alongside flowers and floristry. Some of the advice is good, and none of it is wholly bad, for, dependent upon the location of the shop and its likely customers some of the most unlikely lines *may* be a success in a given area.

Here are some lines that are part of, or near to, the world of floristry, though it must be emphasised that *flowers and floristry* must *remain the core of your business*, and diversifications kept to the sidelines.

Bedding plants and garden supplies

Stock *only* if you have sufficient space for permanent outside display, suitable storage and/or an adjoining yard. Bedding plants which have to be removed from display and brought into the shop can cause disruption of normal work, and dirt and litter in the very part of your shop which should be the most attractive. They create, too, work load, mornings and evenings, for which you may have to take on additional staff. Even in a small way it is not worth the hassle. Further, the season is short and being at the mercy of the weather, is likewise quite unpredictable.

Supplies such as fertilizers, insecticides and similar products are far better left to the garden centre or your local ironmonger. Such items you need to stock are those relating directly to indoor plants, eg aerosol insecticides, small packs of liquid fertilizer, and maybe a few small plastic pots and containers.

Artificial and dried flowers

Flowers which do not die can be sold by anyone, but are far more suited to the trade of the retail florist. However, they should not take charge of your shop, and unless you intend to abandon 'live' floristry forever, they should be limited to significant, but secondary display. They have many uses, all related to the normal trade of the florist.

Fabric flowers, for example, can be used to demonstrate bridal designs in a more or less permanent display. They are useful too in the creation of small giftware arrangements, used perhaps with dried flowers, but perhaps their most important role is in places where no living flowers or plants could be expected to exist for more than a few hours, such as in semi dark situations, in an overheated atmosphere, seated perhaps upon radiators or in a direct line with heating vents.

Artificial flowers have a long history. The relatively crude products which came our way in the first half of the century soon gave way to ingenuity with plastics, and for a period plastic flowers were thrust at us from all sides. They became too popular and lost their appeal, and we had a brief but short-lived promotion of feather flowers to contend with. Perhaps they looked too much like the fair ground, for they never really caught on and soon disppeared as the first of the fabric flowers (silk flowers as they were first called) came in from the Far East. They look like staying, for year by year they improve, become more natural looking in form and colour, and the range widens. Because of their strong similarity to the real thing, they are likely to be with us for some long time.

Dried flowers (and foliages) were expected to supplant them, but dried flowers are a different product, with a different appeal and they do not attempt to imitate any living flower other than themselves. Hence they have a unique attraction for those who abhor the imitation but still need something which is semi-permanent. All too often the dyes used are crude and do nothing to enhance the product. But where the natural colours are retained (although a little dulled), dried flowers and foliages have a place with florists. The extent to which one may stock and use them depends very much upon location and the public who shop in your area. The final decision will rest with you.

Pottery and glassware

Because many flower containers are of pottery, a range of pottery is a natural extension of the florist's stock. Some glassware, too, can be included. The extent to which you move outside the general description of 'containers' will depend upon space available, personal preferences and cash flow. Hardware generally has to be purchased in bulk and because it is not cheap merchandise, it will mop up a sizeable proportion of your ready cash. Rapid sales are somewhat unlikely. Mark-up is usually in the region of 30 to 40% on cost, so you may not see your capital back for a few weeks. These are points which must be taken into consideration. There is one other: if you are situated in a 'shopping parade' or similar centre there may be a protection clause in your lease to the effect that nobody else may sell flowers, whilst you may not sell goods more properly related, perhaps, to the glassware shop which is part of the same complex. You may get away with flower containers, but there could be a limitation upon other kinds of pottery or glassware.

Wicker and cane products

Much that has been said for pottery applies here, except that you can usually buy in far smaller quantities from your sundriesman, and far less capital is involved. You are not likely either to offend any restrictive clauses in your lease unless you extend into wicker furniture. Baskets are a necessity in floristry and a few appropriate examples should form part of your stock-in-trade.

Flower arranging sundries

If you are in an area in which flower clubs exist, you will be wise to establish business relationships with the flower arrangers. Having done so, keep a reasonable stock of the sundries they are most likely to need, eg stem supports, foam, pin cushions, *Oasis fix*, sprays and wires. Whether or not you approve of their activities, there is business to be done with people who use flowers, talk flowers and manipulate flowers. If they do not buy from you, they will buy elsewhere, but with a little patience and a neat display of their likely needs, you can do business and possibly, too, make friends.

Ribbons

Florists' ribbons are part of your own basic equipment. You may be asked to sell lengths of ribbon (or synthetic ribbon) from time to time. This too is business. Ribbon can show a good profit if sold by the metre, but we suggest that you stock only the normal range of florist's ribbons, those which your sundriesman can supply.

Giftware

The term giftware covers a multitude of small items which are usually unperishable, can be carried away easily, are suitable as gifts and are within a price range acceptable to your public. Some small items go well with flowers, many others do not. Giftware sells far more easily in areas that attract tourists, and is unlikely to bring many sales in a non-tourist area. Certainly you will sell some, wherever you are situated, but it is not wise to lock up too much of your ready cash in slow-moving products.

Cards

All florists need cards to use upon gifts, tributes, etc. Not all florists need to have a greeting card department, and it should only be considered if there is sufficient space (wall-space is preferable), and a need to get more people into the shop. Card firms are keen to establish outlets and will make generous offers to bring you into their orbit. Never make a decision on the spot and always look around well before deciding that you can add greeting cards to your stock. If there is a genuine greeting-card shop in your vicinity, maybe you will be wise to say 'no'. But, do not unduly limit your stocks of cards – a change from some of the mini-cards offered to florists might be welcomed by your customers.

Books (garden and flower books), pictures, etc

Neither takes up much room and indeed pictures can enhance a lofty wall. A disadvantage to be overcome is the likely concentration of humidity in an average flower shop. Dampness will ruin books very quickly, and unless very well sealed, can affect pictures. A closed showcase is advisable for books. Approach this form of diversification with some caution. Much depends upon your likely clientele and your display space.

Toys

Small cuddly stuffed animals, teddy-bears and bunnies, may not earn you very much as direct sales, but are often invaluable in adding interest to an arrangement perhaps for a child in hospital, or for the mother of a first baby. They add a touch of individual interest in pleasing the recipient. Other little gimmicks may be used. Bees, butterflies and frogs have been seen and, used with discretion, they can achieve the same objective.

Even less likely diversifications may be offered. Do not be carried away by (maybe) a wish to stock confectionery. Evaluate its likely profits against the space it will occupy, and what that space could earn for you if used for other products. Finally, keep foremost your integrity as a *florist* – that must be your main business.

PART THREE

Sales force in floristry

Flowers will always be wanted but in what volume and from what source? The flower shop is the obvious source of supply. But the shop can succeed or fail miserably if the image is wrong. Display, quality of product, services, publicity, all play their part, but the effect can be ruined if salesmanship is ignored.

Although the following chapters are addressed directly to sales staff, it is hoped that they will also help those with longer experience and wider responsibilities. They can be used as a basis for sales-staff training, and as a check upon current procedures.

Sales staff – who are they?

At some time in our lives every one of us is a customer. Sometimes they call us consumers. Some of us are going to be engaged in selling, and as employers or employees we play our parts, sales persons or, perhaps just plain sales staff. But we do not have to be plain, nor particularly gorgeous. We must, however, be efficient.

Further, we can constantly assess ourselves by watching others. Maybe we shall observe in others our own weaknesses and faults, and experience their effects. Hopefully we shall be able to identify the fog that can creep so easily into the simplest commercial transaction. Will we go back to that shop where the assistant is so dumb, rude, or simply uncaring? Or shall we shop elsewhere, where the assistant was efficient, cheerful and polite? Self-assessment requires that most difficult of activity, that of quiet thought.

Floristry is an industry which relies rather more than most trades upon the efficiency and personality of its sales staff. Our products are perishable and have only a limited shelf life. Because they are living matter, they require servicing whilst held in stock. Thus there is an urgency for sales because the flow of production cannot be halted at the turn of a switch.

Most florists' shops are relatively small businesses, relying very much upon personal goodwill and are rarely of sufficient size to warrant the introduction of formal staff training. Much, therefore, depends upon study of the subject and perhaps personal training of one or two people at a time.

Selling is, in essence, a personal transaction between two people, the vendor and the purchaser. Whilst the techniques of selling are basically the same for all retail trades, it is the *manner* of selling which is so important.

Responsibility

In retailing, the only representative of the industry seen by the customer is, in most cases the salesperson. So that the shop and maybe the whole industry is judged by that person's success (or failure) to inspire confidence. As retailers it is easy to forget that behind us there is the whole floricultural industry, employing thousands and representing the investment of many millions. The sheer skill, the romance and many imponderables that lie behind the production of a perfect rose are never seen, nor but rarely thought of by the public. But the retailer is *seen*, and must represent the whole. One further point. The income upon which the industry depends comes from but one source – the customer. Thus we sell, YOU sell on behalf of the whole. The customer you serve is, indirectly, employing you. And NOTHING – nothing at all happens until somebody sells something.

Confidence

To inspire confidence in others you need to have confidence in yourself. Confidence is based very much upon knowledge. How much interest are you willing to take in flowers and the flower industry? Are you willing to learn? It is not necessary to start with any great wealth of knowledge. You can build as you go. The materials are all about you as you work – the flowers, their varieties and origins, seasonal changes, packaging, flower and plant care and behaviour. Ask questions, and continue to ask so that you can begin to build a picture. Keep a notebook and read all the trade publications that you can lay your hands upon. If your employer does not take any, subscribe or buy them for yourself. When possible, attend meetings and lectures relating to floristry. Seek help from those who obviously enjoy their work. No one person will know it all, but collective information is there for you to find. Take nothing for granted however. Discuss your work and responsibilities with your employer, and keep in line with his or her wishes. Remember, too, that you will never finish learning, and today's wisdom can become 'old hat' in a very few years time.

Look in the mirror

Those with inborn sales ability are rare. Most of us have to learn, and the most valuable attribute we can wish for is an enquiring mind. But we do not see that in the mirror. We see ourselves, as we are, and as a customer might see us.

Differences in temperament will not be seen so clearly and they must be sorted out within ourselves. Some of us are gregarious and love meeting people whilst others have to overcome an inborn shyness. You, and only you know your own characteristics, and their control is in your hands. Either extreme can be a disadvantage.

If you are a friendly person and can converse easily, you will enjoy meeting people in your business life. Most of them you will like – but a few you may not. Remember that a customer is still a customer and you must keep your head in all circumstances.

Your sales personality matters a great deal. The need to be sympathetic to the bereaved, kind to the elderly and the worried, considerate to the deaf and lighthearted with the wedding party. Most customers will be as fit and able as you are, but they still appreciate a word of welcome and smile when they approach. If you can remember a customer's name, use it, and get off to a flying start. People like to be recognised.

Cultivate a calmness of speech and avoid ever sounding doubtful or disinterested. If you cannot find an answer to a question, admit it and say clearly 'I don't know but I will find out for you'. Positive action is often all the enquirer needs.

Patience will be needed especially for those who are slow in making a choice. Retain a sense of business; a sense of proportion in how far you can allow a conversation to wander from the purpose of the visit; how soon to clinch a sale or an order; when to steer, and when to wait. Above all, *lead* your customer but never, never drive.

Personal appearance

Do not be downcast if age or looks seem to weigh against you. If you are lucky they may both be on your side. If you think you have a problem, remember those who have made good in public in spite of all sorts of physical problems. As for age, we know plenty of really charming folk who will never see sixty again.

A pleasing tone of voice is a useful asset. One that can convey laughter or sympathy with equal ease. If you have a dialect, or accent, stick to it. You may get your leg pulled, but you will be remembered. Always speak clearly and look your customers in the eye.

One's appearance should be neat, clean and attractive. As a customer I am sometimes appalled at what I see. For the ladies, a neat hair style is preferable. Acceptable up-to-date style if you wish, and can afford it but, please, neatness. If facial make-up is used, it should be applied skilfully and properly suited to the wearer. Take care with your teeth and with your breath; there are remedies in every chemist's shop. Take equal care with your hands and fingernails. Although some of your work may be dirty and hard on the skin, there are many creams and lotions that will preserve their appearance and softness. Use perfume in moderation only, and wear the minimum of jewellery.

Overalls and working jackets should be clean and in good repair. Some dirty jobs may have to be done in the background, but it is no problem to protect your clothing, and it is advisable to keep a second overall for such duties. Even your shoes will be noticed. High fashion rarely goes with comfort, and neatness is essential. Remember too the safety factor – soles that may slip easily on a damp floor are not recommended.

Men, too, should be particular about appearance. They may have to perform some of the heavier work within the shop, but there is no need to advertise that fact to a customer. Undervests, collarless shirts and perspiration are out of fashion. No customers expect a salesman to look pretty, but he should look wholesome, tidy and businesslike. The barber's shop and the drug store can help over most problems of personal hygiene. In general, a cotton or nylon jacket takes the place of an overall, but it should have ample pockets and room for an extra layer beneath in cold weather. In summer, a short sleeved shirt of modest colour and pattern with breast pockets is generally acceptable. (Braces, by the way, are NOT in fashion).

Qualifications

Advanced educational qualifications are not essential for good selling, but where they exist will give an added impetus to a career. All that is learned at any stage at school or college is useful, even Latin, seemingly a dead language, springs to life and usefulness when dealing with botanical names.

Writing must be clear and easily legible, and keep in mind the fact that *others* may have to read what you have written. The order taken today will have to be executed by someone else if you are away ill tomorrow. Arithmetic, day to day accounting, should have the same degree of care and accuracy. Modern tills and pocket calculators will perform the more complicated sums, but some mental agility is needed when packing orders to their correct value, or estimating the value of flowers to be used in a design.

All of this is the background to being READY TO SELL.

Preparedness

Perhaps nothing makes a worse impression upon a customer than an air of slackness, or unreadiness. However, Utopian tidiness and preparedness are conditions which are hard to maintain in a busy shop. Hence, more responsibility is thrown upon the salesperson – the one who, however great the confusion around, however early or late in the day, must be ready to meet the customer.

Preparedness is as much a physical duty as a state of mind. Punctuality is part of it, and nothing is worse than the customer having to encounter a saleslady who is still combing her hair ten minutes after the shop is open.

It is undeniable too that friendly relations between all members of staff and management are desirable, and tend to create a good atmosphere that a customer can sense. But the morning's personal conversations should be sorted our *before* the shop opens, or postponed until later. The average customer has come into the shop to buy, or to order flowers and will not be interested in last night's play on TV, pop-ratings and football results. Any tendency to allow personal conversation to delay or disrupt the act of selling is wrong. The customer must have precedence over your time and attention.

Similarly, eating, drinking, chewing and smoking have no place in salesmanship. Enjoy your coffee, your bun and maybe your cigarette in private and away from the sight of your customers. Take a break when it is allowed, and do not make a martyr of yourself by refusing to stop when told. Self-pity has no place in business. Allow nothing to insulate you from meeting your customers. They pay for your fullest attention.

Being prepared is not simply a matter of standing around until something happens. Preparedness means knowing your stock, its prices, its sequence in selling and how it can be used. Plant and flower display may not be your sole responsibility, but its maintenance certainly is. In fact there is a degree of tidying to be done after almost every sale.

Always be ready with the tools of your trade. Pen, pencil, order pads, knife and scissors, paper, bags, staplers, pins, tying string, ribbons and adhesive tape. Cards, too, for customer's and for your own use. Make out a daily price list and keep a copy alongside the telephone. If others are working with you, or for you, make sure that they have all the information that may be needed.

Self-confidence

Self-confidence will grow with experience and efficiency. First, however, a warning. Beware of over-confidence. The pushing, hurrying and booming personality may be encountered in doorstep selling and perhaps in the street market, but it has no place in a flower shop, where a quieter, attentive confidence is necessary. What is most important is that the customer should have confidence in you. He or she, meeting you for the first time, will have no idea of your qualities. So it is through the greetings and the overtures to a sale that you have to make contact.

Never allow a customer to feel neglected or unseen. However busy you may be, possibly with another customer, it costs nothing to say 'Good morning, I'll be with you in a few minutes'. And, as you say it *smile* a welcome. Make sure too that the greeting is appropriate to the time of day and the kind of day. (Some elderly hero having plodded through pouring rain may not agree about the *goodness* of the morning but there are other greetings.)

The customer's response may give you the first clue about the sort of sale that you will be conducting (a bunch of daffodils, a funeral tribute, a bouquet?) If your first cast fails, tread carefully for you may have a customer needing all the tact and perhaps sympathy that you can offer. There is usually a reason for preoccupation, and bereavement is the most common cause.

Maybe your customer is deaf. Mostly, however, those so afflicted use a hearing aid so you need not shout. Let a deaf person *see* you speak, for many can lip-read, and speak rather slowly and smile with your eyes. Whatever the situation, be prepared to enter into the mood of your customer. Some will come to you as merry as others are sad. Some are worried and some could not care less. Births, deaths, marriages, birthdays, celebrations, anniversaries or just 'some flowers for mum'. They will all come your way sooner or later.

You may have to give guidance or suggestions about card messages, about the suitability of certain flowers for certain occasions, even about the location of an address, particularly if it is a relay order. Keep an eye upon the customer selecting his own card, particularly if he is not familiar with English. ('Loving Memory' is not appreciated on a birthday, nor is 'Bon Voyage' at a funeral.)

Never get impatient and say 'How much do you want to spend'. You might get the answer once received from a Yorkshireman 'Nowt'! Keep your conversation and choice of words as fresh and sincere as possible. Avoid the stereotyped if you can, and 'Have a Nice Day' has reached comic classification, and can only be used in satire. Your speech is the indicator to your personality and to the interest that you have in your work. If an expression fails to please you, search for something better: words that have meaning and honesty and that convey your integrity.

The customer who comes back, and looks for you to serve him is the best reward of all.

Selling floristry

Sometimes we are asked, 'Why bother to sell floristry, why not simply sell as many flowers as you can and let the public do the rest?'. The majority of flower shops both sell and display floristry as well as cut flowers. Here and there, there are firms which concentrate on one extreme or the other. There are florists whose whole business is concentrated upon decorative work, and there are flower supermarkets which are designed and operated simply as flower selling depots. Both sides are equally important and necessary to the industry, and both need good salesmanship.

The chances are that you will find yourself selling plants, flowers and floristry. To sell floristry you will need a greater degree of skill and certainly some knowledge (if not practical experience) of the techniques of commercial floristry. (The latter is outside the scope of this book, but is nevertheless an important aspect of your training.)

For selling, there is one aspect which must be fully understood: that of pricing. Floristry, whether it be in the form of an arrangement, a bouquet, a wreath or a corsage, is a professional skill that cannot be provided for nothing. It involves time, space and skilled labour. So, if you are to sell economically you must have a clear understanding of the full cost of each design to be sold. Any arrangement or design sold must be priced correctly.

Actual costings vary between city centres and the relatively country areas. You may not as yet be a qualified florist but, as a salesperson, you will be selling, or taking orders for designs created by someone else. Some floristry is sold over the counter, but far more is sold in response to orders, and it is in this latter context that selling skills are most necessary. You must know what you, or your firm, can produce on a given day, its likely cost, its suitability for an occasion, possible content in terms of flowers and foliage and, most important of all, you must be able to guide and advise a customer whose wishes are vague or, just occasionally, impracticable. You have to be ready with ideas, artistic and economic, and able to explain them helpfully.

Give special regard to the purpose and the location for which an order is being placed. For example, stage presentations should usually be in the form of a presentation bouquet or basket, *without* cellophane wrapping. For receptions and banquets, the formal bouquet is more suitable, light to carry and toning with the colour of a dress to be worn, if known.

Flowers for the patient in hospital are, all too often, sent without any thought of what will happen to them when they arrive. Hospitals are busy places where the nursing staff have little, if any time, to arrange and care for the flowers. Also the patient may be too ill even to remove the paper. In such cases, recommend an arrangement in a small vase or bowl that will sit nicely on a bedside table and, apart from topping up with water, will need little attention. Elementary advice? But how often is it ignored. This is a further chance to sell floristry and flowers – and to please your customer.

Packaging is an important factor, whether the flowers are delivered or taken away at the time of sale. The special pack, incorporating perhaps a box, or cellophane, with ribbon and a pleasing arrangement of the flowers within, has become a feature of modern flower sales.

The art of selling
Flowers and foliages, assembled tastefully in the hand at the will of the customer. A style of selling that may take a little more time, but will certainly sell more flowers. If the customer wishes, the assembled bunch can be tied neatly before being packaged

A customer ordering a design for some special occasion will be helped if you can give him a word picture of the possibilities. Selection guides are available today, issued by the relay organisations, which give beautiful illustrations of floristy and some suggestions upon prices. But it is your words, attitude and interest in the occasion that will give confidence. If possible, only discuss the price when you have collected most of the significant detail of the order, because these are the clues upon which to base your quotation.

Never quote a price that is too low and never mention any minimum price. Using your judgment of the occasion, first describe or show the very best you can do, and quote well in the upper price range. You can still retreat downwards if the reaction is unfavourable, explaining for example that by the use of less expensive flowers (carnations instead of orchids maybe) you will be able to meet the price which your customer is willing to pay.

When you are receiving an order for, say, decorating for some civic occasion, obtain all the possible information about the décor, colouring, lighting and, if possible, some ideas about the architecture. It is usual for the florist or decorator who will be engaged upon the work to see the customer but he or she may be busy elsewhere and you must be able to advise and to convey some picture of what will be suitable for the occasion.

Decorative floristry is a specialised subject, but is one which you will be wise to study and, as far as possible, practise as part of your career. It may well be that when you book your first order of this kind, you have had little practical experience, but your responsibility is clear. You must convey complete confidence in your firm's ability to carry out a thoroughly satisfactory decoration. You must get all possible detail on the lines indicated above and obtain the name and address of the person ordering and ascertain where and to whom the account is to be sent. Check back with the customer on all important details, especially date and time, and then conclude a provisional appointment for your decorator to view the location. On the day, try to get permission either to help with the work or to go along and see the result. This is all part of your essential training, and by personal observation you can increase your knowledge.

Be imaginative in your work. Keep your eyes and your mind open to new ideas and to original thought. For example, you are asked to send flowers to a child in hospital. The lazy way out is to send 'just some flowers'. But how great will be the delight of both child and parents if you send a miniature arrangement incorporating some small toy or miniature teddy bear. If the flowers are for the mother and new baby, find out the name of the child so that the ribbon and the card can be really appropriate. If the flowers are for the mother, perhaps one of those little floral cradles would be acceptable, but whatever you send, put in a tiny posy, even perhaps a bunch of violets for the baby. These thoughts are appreciated and show your real interest in the occasion.

Should the arrangement be for someone who is very ill, or perhaps immediately recovering from an operation, suggest always flowers of light colouring, preferably blue and cream, because the richer colours such as red and orange are too harsh and stimulating. There is also superstition in some quarters about the use of red flowers in hospital.

For those moving into a new house or returning from holiday, *always* advise an arrangement because the recipient will probably have little time to care for unarranged flowers. In fact the *complete* gift is preferable on almost all occasions for which flowers are appropriate. Selling floristry means selling the finished article, not the component parts.

Wedding orders

For as far back as history can reach, and in almost every nation of the world, flowers have been part, and sometimes a very essential part, of the wedding ceremony. This tradition persists in modern life. For the florist, no other kind of order offers so many opportunities for rewarding salesmanship. But there are a few pitfalls, too.

It is utterly essential that before you attempt to take any wedding order you have a thorough understanding of the economics of the subject and the pricing policy of your employer. As you progress, much of this will be left to you and you will become the person who is the answer to any employer's prayer – a salesperson with an instinctive gift for values. But until then, study and discuss the whole wedding flower service that your firm is able to offer so that in any circumstances, you can sell with confidence.

It is necessary too that you know the seasonal fluctuations of the many kinds of flowers that are used for weddings today, their varieties and relative values, keeping in mind always the peak periods and their effect upon supplies.

Wedding fashions, some knowledge of fabrics and a constant interest in design will help you further, and a good working knowledge of these can be picked up easily from regular study of the quality fashion magazines.

Perhaps one of the major problems of booking a wedding order is the all too frequent presence of those who come to advise the bride. The groom is rarely much trouble, but mother can be, and frequently is, a brake on the proceedings and can sometimes disrupt all logical planning.

Most florists specialising in wedding floristry carry a number of sales aids in the form of pictures, design books, photographs of happy brides in previous weddings and sometimes a more elaborate system of coloured slides, either *seen* directly or projected upon a screen. Also useful, though not tolerated in all shops, are specimen bouquets of dried or fabric flowers. All of these will help you in selling and, properly prepared, will give a guide and starting figures for your quotations.

The sequence in which the order is booked is important. Indeed, some florists use a specially designed pad for wedding orders carrying all the appropriate reminders in the most logical order. Potential customers often make enquiries well ahead of the date. Always make a note of the name and address, and suggest an appointment for discussion of the details. A bride coming by appointment is always an advantage to the florist. Fix a time when you are unlikely to be busy or subjected to interruptions. Then, capture if you can the wishes of the bride, her preferences and ideas for 'the day of her life'.

(The booking of the order can take time, another good reason for understanding the economics of the order. How much time it takes will be a measure of your skill in 'handling' folks and, however good you are, you will from time to time meet those who are determined to spend an hour ordering the flowers, come what may. But, your time is costed by your employer, and the economy, or otherwise, of its usage will be evaluated in relation to the nature of the order you have booked.)

All flowers used or worn at the wedding should be part of the overall design. You may have some trouble in getting this point over and you will sometimes lose. But discussion of this will enable you to remind your customers of the many other uses of flowers on such occasions. You will discuss the bouquets for the bridesmaids as part of the main ensemble, but never before or to the detriment of the bride. It *is* her day, tell her so, two or three times if necessary, and she must be the one who has everything just right. The others follow suit. If the wedding is to be in church, suggest a decoration, or, at least some flowers for the chancel. Some knowledge of your local churches and other places of worship is useful – to know what is permitted and when, and the name of the vicar or other official whose co-operation is necessary when decorating the church or chapel.

Another suggestion, sometimes overlooked initially, is that there should be some flowers at home for the family of the bride to enjoy after she has left. As a variation, flowers could be sent to the two mothers *after* the wedding, perhaps even the day after. This is a lovely gesture and very much appreciated. Other ideas include flowers in or upon the wedding cars, buttonholes for all ushers and chauffeurs, table decorations for the reception, cake decoration, and real rose petals in place of confetti. Weddings which include all of these 'frills' are something of a rarity, but a tactful reminder will give no offence and may produce a significant addition to the order.

Cash and credit   Wedding orders tend to produce 'slow payers' and the occasional bad debt, disproportionately to other types of order. Most shops have very clear rules over payment. To quote one: 'Substantial deposit or full payment upon placing a firm order, or full payment upon delivery'. Tough but effective. Be sure that you understand fully your employer's policy upon credit sales, and if in doubt, get a clear ruling.

WEDDING FLOWERS CONTRACT

NAME & ADDRESS

DATE
DAY
DELIVERY TIME
TIME OF WEDDING

TELEPHONE NO.

CHURCH

BRIDE.   DRESS

HEIGHT
&
BUILD

BRIDESMAIDS
COLOUR OF DRESSES

AGES

HEAD-DRESSES

GUESTS' BUTTON-HOLES

CORSAGES

MOTHERS
GRANDMOTHERS
GODMOTHERS

USHERS
&
IMPORTANT MEN

CHURCH FLOWERS

CAKE FLOWERS

THANK YOU BOUQUETS FOR MOTHERS

SIGNED

TOTAL
DEPOSIT
BALANCE

Sutch Florists' Cards Ltd, Bessels Green, Sevenoaks, Kent

Funeral flowers

Those who come to order flowers for a funeral, will be in varying degrees emotionally upset. They will require your kindness and understanding before all else. However, you must not present a miserable or stuffy personality, but rather one which is quietly and efficiently helpful. In particular, be alert to the little things and small services which may help your customers through a difficult session. For example, suggest that you write the cards – they will probably prefer to do so themselves, but the offer will establish your sympathy. For the elderly, fetch a chair, or find a quiet corner of the shop in which they can discuss their wishes with you. Offer a pen and keep a box of tissues near by. If there is a need to telephone for essential details, you should offer to do it for them.

Listen patiently when you are being told about the deceased, because talking will help to overcome the shock. Equally, be patient and perceptive, in not hurrying those in whom emotion is pent up and controlled. Persons suffering from shock do everything a little slower, so give them time to think without hustling or fidgeting. When you are dealing with a family order, find out as soon as you can who is the next of kin, and which is to be the principal design. This design is to the funeral order what the bridal bouquet is to the wedding order; get it exactly right and in line with the wishes expressed and the rest will follow easily.

Cards may be written on the spot or taken away for writing at home, to be returned to you before delivery of the designs. Offer to collect the cards if there are transport problems or if time is short. When this is done, supply a copy of the order with code numbers against each tribute so that the appropriate coding can be put on the back of the card. This must NEVER indicate the price of the tribute, but it will help to avoid the possibility of any error. Avoid the offer to attach the cards at point of delivery because confusion can occur, and your driver is perhaps not a florist.

Take especial care over quoting prices for unusual designs. Rather than make an error you should take advice from a senior, or, if none is there to help you, offer to telephone a final quotation later in the day. It cannot be emphasised enough that there must be NO mistake

SALES FORCE IN FLORISTRY   77

over funeral flowers. There is no second chance in which to correct an error. Immense confidence is placed with you. To this end, always check back with your customers, whilst they are with you, that you have indeed the correct information, especially in relation to the *Day*, *Time* of delivery, the *Nature* of the designs, the *Cards* and the *Address* for delivery.

Guard the confidential nature of the order most carefully and never allow yourself to break this by divulging details of one person's order to another, not even a member of the same family, unless you have permission to do so.

There are no flowers essentially suitable or unsuitable for funeral designs, but be constantly alert for any objections your customer may register; for example, lilies are either loved or disliked. Beauty is in the eye of the beholder!

If you know that you will have a large number of designs for the same funeral, make sure that you have a note of all the card messages and signatures; cards can be overlooked or misplaced when the flowers are displayed and your record may help the worried relatives after the funeral. It will also protect you in case you are accused of overlooking an order.

When you are asked to deliver to the offices of a funeral director, a list of the tributes and the card messages must be delivered with the tributes.

Finally, you may be required to advise upon the suitability or otherwise of a style or size of tribute. Here is an example. A messenger will arrive, or perhaps will telephone you, placing an order on behalf of a local firm of some consequence. The order placed is modest and might appear paltry in relation to the standing of the senders. If you have doubts, a return call to the firm concerned, ostensibly to check some detail on the card, will give you a chance to check the detail with someone in authority. No harm will be done even if it is then confirmed that the order was correctly given.

In this chapter there is little about salesmanship. Not because it has no application here, but because it must never be *seen* to be applied. This aspect of floristry is in fact a service, but it is also part of our trade and, as such, fair and appropriate prices must be applied to the designs we sell. Provided they are reasonable, be guided always by the wishes of the customer, and base your quotations upon fulfilling, as nearly as possible, those wishes.

The provision of funeral floristry is the most delicate operation within the flower industry. It is valuable business but its opportunities for creating goodwill are even more valuable.

Relay orders

Relay orders are those which you book, but because they are for delivery in other towns (or countries), they will be carried out by the florists in those places. The rules of transmission vary between the different relay organisations. However, this is yet another way in which flowers and floristry are sold. Responsibility is, perhaps, even greater, for the order you transmit must be realistic for the florist to whom it is sent. Do not accept an order for flowers which you suspect may be unobtainable at the receiving end. Do not ask for delivery at some impossible time of day. Make sure that the order is transmitted in good time. Use telephone, telex or cable if there is any doubt.

Your customer may ask for the impossible. Your duty is to guide him or her into more reasonable channels, and never promise something which you know is impracticable, because you will be risking disappointment and a complaint. Certain procedures are essential:

1 Write very clearly, using block capitals for all names and addresses.
2 Record clearly the day, date and (if reasonable) time for which delivery is required.
3 Record the detail, fully yet briefly. Take special care over the card details.
4 Take down the whole order in duplicate and give your customer a copy for checking. (This can incorporate a receipt for cash or become an invoice.)
5 Note always your customer's name, address and telephone number.
6 Pass on to the executing florist any additional information that

may be necessary, such as directions, if the address seems vague, nature of the occasion, relationship to the customer, etc.

It is wise not to mention minimum prices, unless asked specifically. Your quotation should give you room to adjust, either way, based upon the reactions of your customer. Charges should be explained clearly. Do not be apologetic about such items but ensure that your customer understands them. Avoid discussing other florists unless it is in terms of praise or recommendation. Make yourself thoroughly conversant with all flower-relay procedures, so that you can turn up all the required information without delay or fuss. Your customer will not mind waiting whilst you look up an address or routing of an order, but he will resent time wasted whilst you are looking for the appropriate book. Make sure that any amendments are posted in when they arrive with you. Dispatch all orders *promptly*.

In flower-relay work, you are the intermediary between the customer and the florist to whom you will send the order. In fact your customer is ordering flowers that he is unlikely to see, from a florist about whom he knows nothing. Spare a thought too for that florist. Ask yourself if the order you are taking is practicable, fair and economic. If it is not you risk a complaint – not just against yourself but against your employer and the relay organisation. The relay florist is not alone, in as much as he expects reasonable business from other florists, he must equally be aware of the other florist's viewpoint.

The incoming order is equally important, and your care in selection, in precise value and quality is, after all, exactly what you expect from the colleagues to whom you send orders.

Some busy city shops encounter difficulty at peak times of the day and at peak periods because relay orders take up just that little more time than selling the equivalent quantity of flowers over the counter. A queue develops and irate assistants have been known to say, 'Come back later'. An easy solution, with 95% success, is to have suitably keyed order pads ready for such occasions. The customer can then record for you all the essential details in a clear sequence. Often, all that is necessary is for the cashier to check the details, charge accordingly and transmit by 'phone if urgent. Non-urgent orders can be dealt with when the day's peak is over. This can never take the place of good selling, but it is better than disappointing or thrusting out of the shop the customer who wishes to order flowers. Remember too that a relay order is not all yours – some of the business belongs to the member at the other end.

Selling by telephone

Many people coming into the industry today have been using the telephone since the age of two. Yet, however familiar it may be, the commercial use of the 'phone requires more than the experience of casual or family chat. The trained telephone operator must use the instrument so deftly that customers cease to be aware of distance and are able, mentally, to see the person. Cultivate first a clear, not necessarily loud, voice which carries warmth, and a smile. Imply a welcome. Never rush your words, but speak at a normal flowing rate, being careful to articulate clearly upon certain consonants which do not carry well. (F for S, B for P, T for D, etc). Do not allow your tone and volume to die away at the end of a sentence; if anything, give a lift to your voice over the final words. However, be deliberate in giving the details of an order. It will help if you can memorise the recognised spelling code, so useful in the transmission of cables.

Telephone 'code' words
(There are several versions in existence, some using hopelessly difficult place names which are far from easy to remember. In practice, the following version has proved itself)

A	Apple	H	Harry
B	Brother	I	Isaac
C	Charlie	J	John
D	Donald	K	Katie
E	Edward	L	London
F	Freddie	M	Mother
G	George	N	Norman

O	Orange	U	U-turn
P	Peter	V	Victor
Q	Queen	W	William
R	Robert	X	X-ray
S	Sugar	Y	Yesterday
T	Tommy	Z	Zebra

All that has been written already about selling applies equally with the telephoned order. Remember, however, that you can *see* the flowers whilst your customer cannot. This is why your voice and choice of words become so important.

There are certain rules and sequences that will smooth the way of business:

1 Be prepared. Never lift the receiver until you have all ready for use, pen/pencil and pad upon which to write the order or message.
2 Announce yourself without waiting to be asked. 'Hello' is not enough for your caller wants to know if he or she has the right number. It is helpful if you identify your firm and yourself.
3 Find out to whom you are speaking and use his or her name throughout the conversation.
4 If your caller is another florist placing a relay order, there is a laid down sequence in which the information should be passed. If not, and you have a potential customer on the line, the following sequence is suggested:

   (a) Ascertain the DAY and the DATE upon which the delivery is required.
   (b) Ascertain the name and address of the recipient.
   (c) Ascertain the occasion for which the flowers are required.
   (d) Ascertain details of the card message.
   (e) Negotiate and agree the price for the order. Read back to the customer making sure that all charges are fully understood.
   (f) Take customer's full address and name of the person who is to be charged, (and/or operate standard charge-card procedures).
   (g) Obviously all orders placed by telephone are credit sales. Make sure that you are fully conversant with your employer's

policy, and if you are in any doubt, you must ask. The vital subject of payment has to be discussed at some time when you are taking an order, and you must not sound hesitant or uncertain. You must be able to state clearly, and pleasantly whatever terms of settlement are required. If your caller is on any black list (most firms have one) suggest that the cash be sent to you by messenger so that you can proceed with the order.

(h) A caller may ask to speak to your employer, personally. You must find out his or her name and if possible the nature of the business before you ask the caller to hold. Do not reveal the fact that your employer is around – say rather that you will *see* if he is in. This gives him the option of being 'out' if he has no wish to receive the call.

(i) Speak always with a smile in your voice. Beware of implying any sort of 'freeze', however busy you may be. Never erect barriers between yourself and a potential customer, and however stupid he may seem, never make him feel 'in the wrong'.

(j) The things that should always be within reach of your telephone are:
   Message pad, and/or order pad and at least one pen
   Today's price list
   Relay membership list and directory
   Your book of dialling codes
   Your list of 'no credit' customers
   A calendar
   A short list of emergency numbers: doctor, hospital(s), funeral director(s), crematorium, police, ambulance service, post office, fire brigade, etc.

(k) Any orders to be telephoned out should be prepared carefully beforehand, and all details checked. Any stumbling can produce those 'errors of transmission' that we hear so much about. Always insist that the receiving florist reads the order back to you before you are disconnected.

(l) If you need to send a cable, or to use Telex or any other form of electronic transmission, remember that every word counts and can cost. Write out the whole message which you have to send and then look at it carefully to see if there are any unnecessary words. Eliminate those which have no direct bearing on the message.

(Note, however, that Telex, and Messenger, the system now coming into use by Interflora members, each have individual rules for operation. Study the system that you will be expected to use and perfect yourself. Like computers, such systems can only do as they are told by the person operating them. If they seem to be stupid it is more than likely the fault of the operator.)

Care and rotation of stock

The extent to which you are responsible for this will be decided by your employer. In many shops the full responsibility is yours – in others, control is exercised at a higher level and your duties will be to act upon instructions and report.

Stock must be sold and used in the right sequence, the condition of the flowers being of greater importance than their time of arrival in the shop. You will not be expected to make decisions of this nature until you have had considerable experience, but as the one on the spot you must be observant and co-operative with your employer.

You must draw attention to any lines which, for any reason, are hanging fire, deteriorating, or which in your opinion have proved unsatisfactory or unsaleable. It could be that some flowers have not arrived with you in prime condition. This should be reported at once; also any shortages or breakages. Also you must do everything possible to render the 'odds and ends' of lines usable by creating arrangements for sale, or by use in display.

Clear up thoroughly whenever time permits, as perishable stock can very quickly become untidy. Condense half empty vases, clear away and wash thoroughly the empty ones. All vases should be topped up at least every day, and certain thirsty subjects more often. Particularly, check each evening, replacing most items within the cooler, and leaving the shop tidy for a clean start the next day.

Regular servicing of stock is a daily operation with which, in a large shop, you may need help, otherwise it spreads over the whole morning and the shop is never tidy for selling, which must have prime consideration.

(See also notes on 'Daily operations in a flower shop' page 30.)

Servicing stock

The amount of servicing and preparation for sale required by flowers varies considerably from season to season. The fundamental rule is that the flowers and plants which you offer for sale must leave your premises in prime condition and ready for immediate use. It is the impact of flowers newly received that matters: the recipient may have neither the time nor the inclination to condition the flowers in the home. No firm of repute will sell stale flowers, and no amount of conditioning will restore a faded bloom. Yet, even those which are in prime condition may disappoint if they have lacked the proper treatment in the florist's hands.

Here are some detailed, yet simple rules for the care of stock:

CUT FLOWERS

Water Clean rain water is near perfect, although in certain industrial areas it may contain a higher percentage of contamination than tap water. However, there is little wrong with tap water, although in certain areas excessive hardness will indicate the presence of salts that are neither useful nor harmful to plant life.

Free oxygen in the water will encourage the growth of bacteria around the stems. It can be largely eliminated if the water can stand for an hour or so, and can be removed even more quickly if the water is warmed to 'tepidness'. Never use dirty water or water that has been used previously for other flowers.

Containers All containers, of whatever shape, size or substance must be cleaned thoroughly between each usage. Hot water with bleach is most effective in killing off all residual bacteria. This principle should be applied as strictly in retail shops, as in the home. Lack of cleanliness has been responsible for the unfounded rumours that flowers can cause infection in hospital or sick room.

Stems When the flower was growing, it was part of the parent plant, and was cared for by that plant, in terms of water, food and in the removal of toxic matter. When cut or harvested, the flower is forced to set up its own system, and free access to water is its first need. This can only be obtained through the end of the stem, therefore it is essential that whatever length of stem you may require, the end is freshly cut or trimmed before it is placed in water. Deep water is not essential, as the flower can only drink through the end of the stem.

The aperture through which the flower will drink cannot be enlarged by the way in which we treat the end of the stem. For example, a hosepipe of 12 mm aperture can only syphon water at a given rate from a static tank. We may open the end of the pipe spread it and split it, yet the flow of water will remain the same because we cannot enlarge the whole length of the pipe. Therefore with flowers a clean but oblique cut is recommended for the ends of the stems. In theory a straight cut is all that is necessary, provided one has a razor sharp knife or scissors. In their absence the oblique cut tends to lessen the risk of blocking capillaries with torn cell matter.

Hammering, crushing, scraping and splitting stems are procedures that are unnecessary, as they tend to leave dead and unusable material attached to the stems, which in turn will encourage the development of bacteria. Bacteria is the enemy that will quickly block the capillaries.

Hard or very woody stems may still be split if desired, but it is more effective to place the ends for a short period in very hot water, which tends to open the capillaries and kill bacteria. It is emphasised that this treatment should be applied only to the extreme ends of the stems, the lower 5 to 7 cm. With stems that can be broken easily a clean break is nearly as effective as a cut. With carnations the break should be between nodules and not at the nodule point itself.

An airlock is often blamed when roses fail to take water. Such can occur in the stem, when the flowers have been cut for several hours and stored dry. Emergency treatment is to lay the roses flat in a bath of cold water for an hour or so. This will allow the airlock to escape and the flower will resume its ability to take up water. Long periods of immersion are not recommended.

Persistent drooping of the heads can be due also to weak stems, usually the result of too rapid development just before harvesting. There is no valid treatment other than immersion as described above, but it will have no permanent result.

Hot water treatment for stems is advised for most hard-wooded and herbacceous subjects. It should NOT be used for carnations, nor for any spring bulb flowers.

Leaves that are likely to become immersed in water should be removed entirely, because they decay rapidly and introduce toxic matter into the water. If no preservative is being used the water should be changed daily. In particular daffodils should be given clean water after the first few hours, during which time they tend to exude a great deal of toxic slime. During this period they should not share a vase with tulips. Stems should be re-trimmed with an oblique cut each time the water is changed.

Tulips may develop an apparent airlock in the stems, this can in certain circumstances be removed by piercing the stems just below the heads with a sharp needle, thus allowing the air to escape. Such treatment is hardly possible on a commercial scale.

Light Sunshine will invariably accelerate the development of the flower, and shorten its life. Good north light is ideal and many cut flowers will tolerate subdued light.

Temperature Flowers will last longer at lower temperatures. Hot dry rooms provide the worst possible conditions, and the draught from an air conditioning system will quickly cause drooping and drying out of both flowers and foliage. However, it must be remembered that the flowers are for the enjoyment of people, and undue emphasis on the above facts will react against usage. One cannot expect one's customers to go and live in a cold, damp cellar just because their roses will last a bit longer down there.

Refrigeration (freezing) This is NOT RECOMMENDED, it will kill most growing flowers. *Cool* storage, however, is allowable and recommended commercially. Customers should not be encouraged to experiment, but the wise use of a cooling cabinet in a retail shop, is a distinct advantage.

Gimmicks In addition to the above there are a number of gimmicks that may or may not have some value:

Aspirin in the water A questionable treatment with possibly some anti-bacteria quality.

Pennies or other copper coins in the water No known value to the flowers.

Sugar in any form Sucrose (specially processed sugar) is used widely as a food additive, but will stimulate bacteria around the stems if used without some germicide.

Fizzy lemonade An expensive way of doing that which a packet of *Chrysal* will do for much less money.

Feeding cut flowers Spring bulb flowers and most other bulb flowers contain adequate food for the life of the flower and no additives are necessary. Roses, carnations, chrysanthemums and most flowers in the herbaceous group, will benefit from a balanced additive. The additive (there are a number of useful proprietary brands on the market) must contain sugar as a food for the flower together with a germicide, or anti-bacteria agent. Use always strictly according to the instructions on the packet or bottle. A daily change of water is not necessary when using a balanced additive.

Many summer flowers and foliages, for example, stocks and common asparagus are liable to very rapid bacterial development on the stems and the water can smell very offensively after only a few hours. A little bleach, about a dessert-spoonful to the average vase added to the water, will control this and, over a short period, will do no harm to the flowers. Do not apply this to more delicate subjects. The same treatment can be used for most foliages.

Fruit Many flowers, particularly carnations, are adversely affected by prolonged proximity or storage with fruit. Apples, pears, tomatoes and oranges are the worst offenders. They give off etheline gas which is toxic and will cause carnations to curl rapidly.

Carnations are also liable to wilt or curl if confined with another wilting carnation. In other words, one dying flower can contaminate the whole vase or box. Remove dead or wilting carnations immediately they are noticed.

Rubbish All workroom rubbish, stems, leaves, old flowers, petals etc, should be removed as soon as possible away from living flowers. All decomposing matter is liable to give off toxic gas, which can affect your stock and cause further waste.

Fresh air Clean air in a cool well-ventilated room is preferable for all flowers.

Draughty positions should be avoided, especially if the incoming air current is excessively cold or hot (as perhaps from an air-conditioning unit).

Plants

As with cut flowers, the advice here is practical, simple and applicable to most house plants.

The range of subjects is wider than with cut flowers. So, however, is the degree of tolerance in the well grown plant. Therefore generalisation is possible, though we include a short list of subjects requiring specific variations in treatment.

Light Strong North light is most beneficial, and window ledge situation or its nearest equivalent is recommended, unless the room faces predominantly South. If this is the case, care must be taken to avoid scorching by sunshine which will increase growth rate too, and encourage unshapely development of the plant. In South facing rooms it is wise always, to position the plants out of the line of direct sunshine.

Window ledges can be very cold in the depth of winter, and plants can be damaged by contact with frosty panes. A radiator immediately below the window can cause rapid drying out and scorch damage, if the leaves overhang into the room.

Temperature Whilst plants are raised in conditions of ideal temperature and humidity, marketed plants will have been hardened and are tolerant of the conditions most suited to human occupation, ie temperatures of around 15–16°C.

Plants will tolerate higher temperatures too, but will need more frequent attention and particularly more frequent watering.

Lower temperatures, down perhaps to 4 to 7°C will do little harm, provided the plants receive less water. If the plant is going to be unusually cold for a period, cut down watering to the absolute minimum.

Humidity Humidity as is prevalent in a greenhouse, is impracticable in our homes. Plants will adapt to a drier environment without much trouble provided conditions of light, temperature and water are observed. They can be helped too, by frequent sponging or spraying with clean water. When open gas fires are in use, a bowl or dish of water permanently in the room will add back some of the lost humidity.

Water More plants are killed in the home through over-watering than from any other cause. Over-watering and particularly the accumulation of surplus water round the root system, is almost invariably fatal. Every plant should be checked daily, using the finger tips and touching gently the surface of the soil. If it is wet or noticeably damp, no water is needed. If it is dusty, crumbly and gives no sense of moisture at all, then it is time to water.

Clean rain water is ideal, brought up to room temperature when the weather is cold. Tap water contains slight impurities but is usually suitable as an alternative for most subjects.

Generally, water should be applied from the top filling the pot to the brim. If there is little room between the brim and the soil surface, repeat the process so that the root ball can become fully saturated. Plants may also be watered from below, by immersing the pot in water until the bubbles have ceased to rise. Then, in each case make sure that the plant is not going to stand in a puddle of surplus water. Allow all surplus water to drain away, or if the plant is standing in a container of any sort make sure that the flower pot is raised above any possible puddle. A 12 mm layer of sand, gravel or peat in the bottom of the container will usually prevent this happening.

Watch the general health of the plant. If the leaves are limp, discoloured and the growth is retarded, it could be that it is getting too little water. If the leaves are fleshy and tend to show yellow spots, it is possible that it is being watered too often.

All plants grow more slowly in winter, some actually stop any development for several months. At such time they will require far less water.

Always water thoroughly, a few drops on a plant that is nearly dry, will be wasted and may run straight through and out of the bottom of the pot.

There are many stories about communicating with plants – of singing and talking to them and of their imagined reactions. So far, there has been no scientific evidence that plants are the least bit interested in what we say or do. Except, however, to the extent that if we are going in for a chat or sing-song we will also check with our finger tips to see if the plants need watering.

Standing out in the rain is a gimmick that can only succeed if the weather is mild, the rain is gentle and we keep neither cats nor dogs in our garden. Otherwise NO. Cold tea, beer dregs, cigarette ends and discarded party snacks, all are of no particular use to the plant.

Feeding Use only recommended plant food and in accordance only with instructions on the bottle or packet. Liquids are easier to apply to plants in the home.

Re-potting Plants rarely require re-potting immediately after purchase. Indicators that re-potting is needed are:
A general falling off of health in the plant.
Unusually quick drying out of the root ball.
Roots coming out from the top of the pot.
Complete imbalance between the size of plant and its pot.
The plant bursts its pot.

Re-potting should take place at the time of year when the plant is growing more rapidly, ie in the months of April through to August.

Let the expert re-pot for you or do the job yourself by first obtaining a pot which is just one size larger than that which the plant occupies now, and a small bag of the appropriate house-plant compost. With clay pots, a pebble or two or some broken pot to cover the hole is required. With plastic pots no crocks are necessary. Pot firmly and water well immediately after.

Cleaning and leaf-shining Plants with large leaves should be sponged regularly with clean water, adding if desired a little leaf shine or similar proprietory compound. Never use milk because animal fat will tend to clog the stomata of the leaves.

Pests The common Aphis or green fly in one of its several forms is the most frequent unwelcome visitor, usually taking charge of the soft new growth on the tip of the plant. Spray with a pyrethrum based insecticide taking care to smother the whole plant in a gentle mist. Aerosols are particularly useful. Repeat the dose after a few days in case some eggs have hatched since the first spraying. Never use dangerous greenhouse or garden sprays within the home, where they might contaminate food and affect children and pets.

Holidays If there is nobody to care for your plants whilst you are away, try this procedure. Place a piece of thick felt or an old towel in the bottom of the bath, place the plants upon this and allow about 4 cm of clean cold water into the bath. Most of this will drip away during the first few days, leaving the plants standing on a saturated mat, and because of their near proximity to each other creating their own atmosphere of humidity. This is not the perfect answer, but in a surprising number of cases it has worked.

Movement It is not always possible to find the right place for a plant when it is first brought into the home. You may have to experiment with two or three different situations. Having found one in which the plant prospers, leave it there, as constant changes of light value and other conditions are not beneficial.

As with cut flowers, cool well ventilated rooms are favourable, and direct draughts should be avoided.

Special subjects

Cacti and succulents Plants in this group are able to store water and can live quite happily without being watered for several months at a time. For example, cacti are plants of the desert, they have to take up a lot of water in a short space of time, and then live on it for a long period. In the home similar treatment will yield the best results, give them a period of being well watered, probably in the spring or summer months, after which they can be allowed to dry out for some months at a time, particularly if they are in cool conditions. A little water daily is virtually useless. Water very well and then allow a period of dryness.

Ferns Ferns require more water than most house plants and must have a shady or north light position with no sunshine. Be generous with water, never allowing a fern of any sort to dry out completely. Frequent spraying with clean water will be beneficial.

Flowering plants Most flowering plants will respond very well to the treatment advised for house plants generally. However, make sure that water is not dropped or sprayed upon the flowers. Be particularly careful with cyclamen and *never over-water*. Neither should water be allowed to accumulate in the cup shaped corm of the plant, which will be found in the centre of the pot. This will cause rapid deterioration of the plant.

Neither cyclamen nor azaleas should be kept in hot rooms; each plant will prosper in more temperate conditions. Azaleas, however, need plenty of water yet with good drainage; they must never be allowed to dry out.

Use rainwater whenever it is available.

Saintpaulia (or African violets) will prosper if they are standing on a damp medium of peat, sand or gravel. They need strong light, short of full sunshine, and enjoy the kind of steamy atmosphere which may be found on a shelf above the kitchen sink, or on a warm ledge in the bathroom. If they are standing on a wet medium of sand, gravel or peat they will require very little water from the top. Never allow water to fall upon flowers or foliage.

Much of the above advice, and more, will be found in the many plant books that are available today, also upon plant care labels. This simplified version will be found useful.

In summer and in hot, dry weather, thirsty subjects such as hydrangeas and astilbe may be stood in a saucer of water for a day or two, but no longer.

Display the plants in places where they will receive as much light as possible, short of full sunshine.

Some or all of the above advisory information may be found in Care leaflets, available for distribution to the public. Should you be unable to obtain these, a personal flower-care leaflet can be based upon these notes.

Packaging and wrapping

It is essential that any goods purchased, or sent home, should be packed adequately and if possible, attractively. Dust, rain, cold or heat from the sun can damage delicate blooms, and it is important also to protect your customer's clothing, or car, from damage by dripping stems and damp flowerpots.

Flowers that have been conditioned will have wet stems, and an inner wrap is sometimes necessary before finishing the pack with the firm's best paper. Pack efficiently, but with economy. Too much paper can be as much of an embarrassment as too little. Tie the package firmly if there is any risk of the paper loosening, and seal all flaps with adhesive tape.

For the normal day-to-day purchases, the 'cone' wrap is most usual. By placing the flowers diagonally across the paper, with their heads 15 to 20 cm from the corner, you will leave sufficient flap to be turned over and sealed with a pin or *Sellotape* as the final motion. In this way the flowers are protected and nothing can fall out if held upside down, (the angle in which many customers prefer to carry flowers.)

Spare a thought for your customer, too, when he collects from you a special arrangement, or a gift wrap. The average man will just hate having to carry this uncovered, even if only to his car. So make sure that this parcel is fully protected and covered either by clever use of wrapping paper or, better still, in a box. There are many and varied boxes available to the retailer today.

The fibre-board boxes in which we receive flowers today can be put to many uses. But do not use them in their raw state. Suitably

The cone pack
Size of paper, approximately 75 cm × 50 cm
Place the stems nearly to the edge of the paper and rather less than halfway from the lefthand corner. Angle the bunch towards the top lefthand corner. To start, take the lefthand corner over the stems of the flowers, then roll the whole bunch towards the right. With the cone complete, the top flap may be turned over the heads of the flowers and sealed with tape or stapler. Plants may be packed by the method shown here

covered, such boxes can be made very attractive. Use wrapping paper provided it is of sufficiently high quality and preferably carrying the name of your firm. Even better, and to make a really beautiful presentation box, use gift wrapping or foil-faced paper. Seal in place neatly and as a final touch, add a bow of ribbon outside.

Take particular care when placing the flowers within the box, ensuring stability by padding with tissue and, if the price permits, making central tie of narrow ribbon for effect. This is a simple form of gift-wrap and for which a small charge can be made.

However, the value of box packing is never greater than at peak periods when the packed orders can be stacked one on top of the other within the delivery van or whilst awaiting delivery. They handle better too, and save much time and worry for the hard-pressed driver as he runs in and out of gates and up and down innumerable flights of stairs. Indeed, it is only when you have staggered up four flights of draughty stairs in some apartment block, carrying a spreading and perhaps floppy parcel of flowers, that you begin to realise the value of box packing.

Peak periods bring other problems too, and you will find that you or those assisting you have to spend a considerable portion, if not all of the day, packing orders. Quite apart from the time factor, it is essential that you keep this operation away from the customers who still require your service for shop sales, and whose business you need – all day. A packing department well away from the selling area is desirable if there is sufficient room. Discuss this suggestion with your employer.

Card care

Most shops offer cards of all kinds, either for sale at a nominal cost or free to customers. The card message on the order which is delivered is of tremendous importance and often you will be required to write that card. Remember that it will be read by someone who may be ill or distressed, or over-excited and who will in any case be quite unfamiliar with your writing, so write very clearly. In extremis, type the message or use neat block capitals rather than risk it being misread.

If your customer decides to write the card, make sure that he has some clean space upon which to spread himself and write, and please, grant him a moment's peace in which to think what he is writing. Never hover or show impatience but be ready with an envelope into which you put the card as soon as he relinquishes it, without reading it. Mark the envelope with the address at once, or identify it with the order.

In packing, the card should be either inside the package, preferably attached to a flower or a sprig of foliage, or better still, within an envelope, attached to the parcel and bearing the recipient's name and address. Stick the envelope to the package with *Sellotape* and if you use a pin or stapler instead, make sure that you pierce *only* the envelope and *not* the card as well. A card can be precious, never disfigure it.

It is of particular importance to see that cards on funeral tributes can be read easily and when the tribute is from a firm or from a number of individuals, it is easier for all if the message is typewritten onto the card.

Never, in any circumstances, use either a greeting or memorial card as an address label by scribbling the recipient's name and address on the back. The card is a most important part of the order, and if its detail is overlooked by the recipient, you will receive a complaint.

Use the appropriate Care Card for every order intended as a gift, and for all significant purchases within the shop. The value of these cards has been proven by both public comment and a marked lessening of the volume of complaints, many brought about by lack of understanding of the needs of flowers and plants.

Cash and credit

All who handle cash and credit have great responsibility, first to their employers and then to their own characters. Intentional dishonesty is a rarity. Carelessness, appearing to be dishonesty, is, regrettably, found more often.

To protect your own good name, be honest, think honestly, take great care and keep to the rules of your firm. If you have never been told the latter, find out what they are, or in their absence, what procedures are traditional in the firm. Learn them, write them down if necessary and keep them. It is as simple as that, but many people still fail and lose their characters, not from dishonesty but from a slap-happy attitude over cash.

Not only must you BE honest but you must be SEEN to be honest. Be openly careful in every operation, examine the cash from your customer in front of him and make sure that you have in your hands the exact amount that he thinks he has handed to you. State clearly the total of his indebtedness and the value of the bill or bills he has proffered. Use the cash register and then be equally careful with the change, where necessary counting this out to the customer to check both his and your arithmetic.

Frequently, upon booking an advance order, you will be required to take a deposit. Without question, always issue a receipt on the notepaper or order form of your employer and either keep a copy of the receipt or make an appropriate note upon the order you have booked. Nothing looks worse than an apparently unrecorded payment of cash for a future service. Issue a receipt in respect of payment for ALL advance orders and ALL relay orders.

Credit sales can provide difficulty, but *only* if you are not aware of your employer's policy. You must understand clearly how, when and to whom credit is allowed, if indeed it is allowed at all. If you are in doubt about any aspect of a credit sale, you must refer the matter to management. If no responsible person is present you must take no chances. Remember that if your customer is straight he will appreciate your diligence in the matter, even if he is refused the credit for which he has asked. Much of your success in the latter case will depend upon your manner, firm but conciliatory.

Complaints

Complaints, alas, come to the best run businesses from time to time, though not necessarily through any fault of the firm or its staff. Many are, in fact the result of misunderstanding at some stage, perhaps in the detail of an order, or its date, or nature. These are unintentional faults, for which we are all at risk sometimes. Other complaints may arise from the customer being unaware of the true needs of the flowers or plant which you have sent. Still others may arise from a mistake by someone quite outside your control. But, whatever the cause, at the moment of complaining, you have to receive the complaint, with all the explosive indignation of a disappointed customer. However the complaint is registered, you have one duty: to LISTEN. Steer your outraged customer away from other potential customers, hear the case and take notes of all the essential details. By so doing, you will be SEEN to care, which is the first stage towards putting the matter right.

From here on you must act only within the guide-lines laid down by your employer. It can well be that at this stage the whole matter must be referred to him or to the manager. If, however, limited authority is vested in you, make sure that you understand it, and operate it exactly in accordance with instructions. Your attitude is all important. Be sympathetic and express your concern that any circumstances should have arisen to cause complaint. Never pre-judge, and unless you can clarify the matter by an immediate check upon circumstances within the shop, ask for time in which to make the necessary enquiries. Keep your head even in the face of the most vituperative outbursts and, in the end, you may keep your customer.

Limited authority to deal with complaints is often vested in experienced staff. This can apply when a purchase, perhaps a plant, is brought back to you because it seems to have died. If you have authority to settle relatively small issues of this kind, show care and concern for the problem and, in making any replacement (assuming such is justified) make sure that the recipient understands what has gone wrong and where, perhaps, his treatment has been less than ideal. A tactful approach to problems of this kind will preserve much goodwill.

The individual touch

All that has already been said is important; nevertheless, it is but an introduction to a vocation from which you will derive not only a living but a ceaseless interest. No aspect of your employment will give you greater satisfaction than the daily challenge of selling.

In conclusion, here are a few tips that will help:

DO – remember that bustle is not industry. employ yourself usefully about the shop, but never, never be too busy to sell.

DO – regard every customer as your opportunity and not your cross in life.

DO – be patient with all who for various reasons are less fit than you are, especially those who are encumbered with children and parcels, with those who are carrying a load of worry or grief, with those who are physically handicapped. None is that way from choice so lend a hand, and be appreciated for your sympathy and understanding.

DO – ensure your customer has a fair and balanced deal.

DO – create goodwill, for you, your employer and your industry.

NEVER – create or discover difficulties. Some things may be less easy than others, but let this worry remain *your* worry and not that of your customer.

NEVER – seek to put your customer in the wrong, not even in the minutest detail. One-upmanship has no place in salesmanship.

NEVER – by word or deed disparage your colleagues, your employer, your fellow florists or your industry. This is *your* living and if you destroy its image you destroy your own.

NEVER – underestimate your customer. Nobody likes to be downgraded.

NEVER – assess your customer' spending potential in relation to your own; he may be richer or poorer.

NEVER – allow your customers to see you eating, drinking or smoking, or idling. Keep your good image at all times.

NEVER – allow pets or children, yours or anyone else's, to interfere with the business of the store. In difficulty, a piece of string (for the dog) or a sweet or picture book (for the child).
NEVER – ever say, 'How much do you want to spend?'.
NEVER – say that you do not know and then do nothing to find out. This is called dead-endmanship.
NEVER – confuse high pressure tactics with salesmanship. There are dangers in bullying, or jollying a customer into spending more than he or she can afford.
NEVER – persist in the face of a clearly stated price limit. Just make sure that your customer gets the best value within that limit.
FINALLY – as a shopper yourself, would you like to be served by you?

PART FOUR

Management

The prime duty of management is to manage. The proprietor of a retail shop may be known as 'Director', 'Principal', 'Manager' or just 'The Boss'. Whichever hat is worn, the wearer must bear the responsibilities for all four; everything from the day-to-day organisation of relatively routine matters, to the image and prosperity of the business as a whole, today and in its future.

By tradition, florists have leaned too heavily upon the attractiveness and appeal of their product to produce sales. Also, many florists enjoy their work with flowers *too much*. To the extent that handling and designing with flowers takes precedence over responsibility for the whole business. A further responsibility for the Boss, that of Public Relations Officer, is to ensure that the image of the business is geared to the potential customers of the town or district.

Therefore, directors of businesses need to have a very clear understanding of:

(a) those to whom they are selling goods and services.
(b) the type, or sort of customers they wish to attract
(c) the kind of shop they are operating, and
(d) the kind of goods and services which are offered

Salesmanship must be understood and practised, not only on the shop floor but at every level through to management. Training given is of little use if not backed up by understanding and encouragement. Neither should young members of staff be allowed to drift (ie stand around to watch Nelly in order to train, a sad process that used to last for years). Staff should be paid a fair wage, and should be trained to earn it. All of which may sound grim. But it need not be. A cheerful boss can work miracles of understanding and loyalty.

Other areas of management study include:
Display (a science often confused with window-dressing)
The product mix – are you offering that which the public in your area really wants?
Selling methods – are they right or should you go into cash and carry procedures?
Shop layout – is it effective, or is it wasteful of space and labour?
Peak period planning, profit margins and advertising.

Bearing in mind the need to know the type or sort of customers you wish to attract it could be advantageous to study the changes that have taken place in retailing over the last ten years. The cash and carry, supermarket style of selling – the alleged time-saver which still produces queues of people waiting at check-out – brings a very high turnover. Such a system will not fit into a traditional flower shop, neither, from recent observation, does the flower shop fit well into the supermarket. Yet, do we do enough to encourage brisk cash and carry sales? A few buckets of daffodils left out in the wind on a spring day are not likely to bring in much business, for the stall-holder down the road can do the job a great deal better. But flowers ready for quick sales within the shop – bunched perhaps and wrapped, carrying a clear price ticket and of high quality – advertised by a window announcement and with 'specials' or weekly 'special offer days', cannot be ignored. It may not bring in much the first time it is tried, but it can build . . . and build. Nothing is wasted for the bunches can be made up from stock, a few at a time, or aqua-packed ready-for-sale flowers may be bought specially for this trade (but these may be sold elsewhere in your area whereas *your own* packs carry some individuality.) Make sure that the contents of a pack will in fact be *of use* to someone wanting to make a tasteful arrangement in a vase (and not some unlikely combination of both colour and variety.) Your sales staff must be prepared for this style of business. It presents little difficulty to those with experience of peak-period selling, and requires only a sense of urgency coupled with breezy courtesy.

It is wise to take a hard look at your 'style' of trading. If you are aiming at the mass market – the quick sales of considerable quantities of low priced flowers – are you in the right location? Or are you in an up-market place where £25 and £40 arrangements may be the order of the day. The two styles do not mix easily, and if you are offering the wrong mix, or the wrong image, it could be holding back your profits.

Display

Responsibility for the planning and designing is with management. By sensible delegation, trained staff can take over such duties, often achieving results which surpass the suggestions of the boss. The first rule is to discuss all display plans with those who will be carrying out the work and its maintenance.

A comprehensive display of goods is essential. Display will catch the eye and should draw attention to the qualities of the product and/or the services offered. Primarily a display feature should attract attention. Fuller information, prices perhaps, should be in the vicinity.

In some trades it is possible to establish a clear definition of display as opposed to window dressing. In the flower shop it is not so easy, and the elements of good display are essential whenever we offer our produce to the public. Plain window-dressing showing a parade of well filled vases in serried rows went out of fashion a long time ago and is rarely seen today. Our windows (our outward aspect) have to incorporate the best of both worlds – a vending showcase and a display that can capture public attention.

Pure display still has its place, however, particularly when time, space or special occasion allows for creative design without any hampering strings of daily selling or accessability attached. Frequently such display windows are planned for week-ends, public holidays, and are used with great effect for festive or commemorative occasions.

For the rest of the year, a pleasant but sometimes uneasy compromise must take place. If our display is composed of our stock in trade, we have to be sure that everything is accessible. One must avoid the situation in which it is necessary to remove four vases and crawl on all fours to reach a bunch of violets from the front of a window! Display must be flexible and adjustable to the needs of the hour. A good day's trading will produce gaps from which plants and flowers have been sold, so constant tidying and filling will be necessary. The display must not impede or reduce by much the floor space, especially at peak periods when rather more people will, we hope, be around. At such time, it should extend upwards rather than spreading on the floor, where damage can so easily occur. (It is not unknown for valuable stock to be knocked over, trodden upon and, in one hilarious incident, sat upon by an elderly and slightly off-balance shopper.) Keep all choice and valuable stock out of the reach of inquisitive children.

All flowers and plants offered for sale should bear a price-ticket. The ticket should be printed clearly, visible to the public and to sales personnel. A number of firms offer price-ticketing systems, of varying usefulness. With wire, strong white card and an ability to write clear bold figures, an inventive florist may decide to create a personal system. The essential factor is clarity, in both naming the variety and its price, but the ticket should not detract from the display by being too large, or gaudy in colour.

Plants can present a problem when you have, for example, azaleas at several differing prices. Whilst a small wooden or plastic ticket thrust into the soil can be read at close quarters, it can rarely be seen by a potential buyer. A composite ticket stating the range of prices for azaleas may be the best example, though the smaller ticket should be retained on each plant.

Small cards on plastic sticks can be most useful, plus a displayed price list – perhaps upon the inside of the window, giving all the main plant prices for the day. There may be other solutions but the principle is that the customer must see the produce and be able to understand the prices.

Windows

Shop windows provide you with a view of the passing world. They provide the public with an image of the business being conducted therein. At least, they should. They can draw and attract the public to the shop, or repell with clutter, gimmicks, posters, litter and empty buckets. (Sometimes even, at weekends, a drawn blind!) Care for display, its planning and execution is a never ending drill in a busy shop, and demands attention from anyone not for the moment engaged with a customer. ('Anyone' meaning staff *or* management.)

Effectiveness depends not upon the volume of produce crammed into a given area, but upon the quality of the produce and the manner of its display. It may emphasise something in season, something which needs some publicity, a Christmas or Easter theme, or maybe a wedding spectacular. Local occasions can often supply a theme: a Royal visit perhaps, or a sporting event, not forgetting the peak days such as St Valentine's and Mothering Sunday.

A window can be screened to give emphasis to a spectacular design or, as is more often seen today, the whole of the shop becomes the display area, lit at night by carefully situated spot lights. In effect this means that the shop window is left wholly or nearly clear, to give the best possible view of the interior of the shop.

If the shop is in a busy street there are immense opportunities for publicity at relatively low cost. Often you can make use of flowers that are too advanced for sale and which otherwise would be wasted. Shops situated in closed precincts do not have this advantage after closing hours. Nevertheless the need for effective display at all other times is just as great.

Lighting

A combination of fluorescent and tungsten lighting is found to be most effective in most flower shops. The fluorescent tubes should, if possible, be screened, and avoid particularly their unscreened use in the shop window where they dazzle rather than illuminate. You will be offered colour fluorescent lighting, such as is used to enhance certain colours of goods in other trades, but be very careful, for that which enhances one colour will kill another and in floristry we need full colour range illumination. White, or warm white fluorescent with tungsten bulbs as spots is the best combination seen to date.

Lighting is, however, an important part of display, and in planning your premises, be sure to include some adjustable spot lights, both in the window and throughout the shop.

The sales area

Flexibility

For those who are planning for a new store, one word of advice will relieve many a heartache. Avoid, whenever possible, creating *fixtures*. Counters, desks, wrapping areas, cash desks and tills, display fittings and even some lighting – all of these should be moveable and capable of adaption to seasonal variations or changes in trading emphasis.

True, one cannot push out walls at will, neither can one make day-to-day adjustments to partitioning and windows. But everything that is within the shell of the shop will serve you best if it can be mobile and capable of conforming to your needs, which must, if you are alert, vary from time to time.

A daily turnabout is not advisable but assessment at fairly frequent intervals is recommended. You should not require teams of removal men and decorators to make a shop a more convenient place in which to do business.

Pride and prejudice

No businessman is without his pride, and quite a few of us nurture some prejudice somewhere in our natures. Thus changes within our shops are not always regarded with enthusiasm.

We have pride in our discernment as business operatives. Pride in our premises and trading image, and pride in our judgement and industrial knowledge. We are even known to have prejudice about the traditional nature of our particular kind of trading, about our divinely endowed capacity to be right. 'I may have my faults', says a popular poster, 'but being wrong is not one of them'.

But if you have read thus far without throwing the book away in disgust, step inside your shop (preferably when no-one else is there) and look around. Pay particular attention to the following key points. Study their location as well as their furnishing. Think of their functions in normal trading conditions. Are they capable of adjustment at peak periods? Do they add to the decor and efficiency of the shop – or are you carrying them?

Key points

(a) Display and customer space.
(b) Cash control.
(c) Wrapping and packing area.
(d) Management or shop desk.
(e) Customer writing desk/relay order area and, if possible,
(f) Comfortable interview room for booking wedding and funeral orders.

You may have good reason to be pleased with what you see: evidences of durability, solid workmanship, systems that have stood the test of time; a business that is valid and a shop which echoes part of yourself; space in which to do some of the work you most enjoy. Yet we can all take refuge in the glow of past successes, and hide behind the axiom that states (with perfect truth) that change for the sake of change does nobody any good.

If we are wise we will walk quietly through our premises from time to time and take stock of the situation. Are we nursing any fallacies? For example, our premises may have served us well for twenty years without need for change. Twenty years of good trading conditions; can we look forward to another twenty years with equally good prospects?

Maybe we are traditionalists. We inherited the shop like this and we like it this way. Do we know whether our customers and staff share the same opinion?

The shop easily becomes crowded, especially at peak selling times. We like to be seen being busy. Do our customers enjoy waiting? Are we not driving them into the arms of our competitors?

Changes may offend some of our older customers. Have we given thought to those who enjoy changes, those who will enjoy shopping in improved conditions and the inquisitive folk who perhaps have never been into our shop before?

We cannot afford expensive equipment. Yet expense is relative to the degree of necessity. Essential replacements and genuine improvements will soon pay for themselves. Neglect is the most costly form of mis-management.

Changes will take up our time and may disrupt habitual tempo of our business life. Are we in business for profit or as a pleasant relaxation. Those who go bust have too much time on their hands.

This shop is too small and cramped. No alterations can increase our space. If we can admit that we are cramped in this shop, we should be considering an extension or the possibility of removal to more convenient premises.

We have only a short lease here and improvements will mostly benefit the landlord. Mobile equipment and furnishings can be taken with you.

Display space

Flowers and plants require space if they are to be displayed effectively. We have discussed display from the angle of sales personnel yet the provision of space within the context of the whole shop is a managerial responsibility.

Where shop windows are to be used for both display and sales, any unnecessary partitioning or 'boxing in' should be avoided. Sales staff need to get quickly to any displayed item and accessability should never be restricted.

Whilst some departmentalisation is desirable, the 'open look' which draws the eyes of the public right into the store, is preferable. Crowded windows or those plastered with advertising announcements have no invitation in their message.

Indoor plants are often displayed separately from flowers, and preferably so for visual effect, easy selection and service. Display groups, rather than one giant display, will allow for this provided there is sufficient floor space. Open, walk-around display groups are necessary if you are to avoid a 'jumble-sale' effect. Shopping should be a gentle pleasure, not an obstacle race.

Take these points into consideration when evaluating space and, when making changes, never allow elaborate fittings or furnishing to dominate. Some types of display furnishing tend to steal the show rather than enhance the products they should promote. Make sure your plants are not lost in a dazzle of mirrors and coloured lighting. Large wall-mirrors are immensely useful for giving a sense of space to small premises. If they fit right down to the ground, make sure that they are suitably screened or engraved, as customers have been known to try to walk clean through a mirror.

Shop doors are sometimes placed very inconveniently, and open in such a way as to impede access to the selling area. If you decide to invest in a complete new frontage, such difficulties should be solved by your surveyor/architect. If you are content with the main frontage, you may still need to make adjustments to the door(s); make sure they never take up useful display space and never get in your customers' way.

Display within the shop is wasted unless the potential customers can see it. They need space from which to look, to browse, perhaps, and discuss an intended purchase. Thus it will be obvious that the maximum proportion of the shop must be given over to what may be called the selling area.

In large premises it is not difficult to create a sense of freedom – of open-planned viewing which customers like and appreciate. It is not so easy in the smaller shops where, in many cases, the only solution is to organise display on varying levels and make the fullest use of height. However, larger premises have their troubles too when stocks are low and empty shelves become too obvious. A few large indoor plants, held in stock, will be useful in covering some of the gaps, whilst removable furnishing, once removed, no longer proclaims the emptiness of the shelves. Mobility and adaptability are the essential factors, whatever the size of your premises.

Cash control

Cash control is generally by the use of the cash register, although in multiple concerns the check-out or cashier's desk is more practical and very much safer. In siting the cash register, three factors must be satisfied: *accessibility* to the staff handling cash; *safety* from the light-fingered or snatch thief; and *economy* in use of space, ie not occupying a space which should be used to advantage for the display of goods.

The accessibility should allow for sales staff to move to and from the till without having to climb over each other on busy days. The height of the unit should be studied. If it is too high, mistakes will occur in registration and change, and those of smaller stature will become rather less efficient after two or three smart blows on the chest from a hard and well-sprung cash drawer. Lighting above the till must be good for accuracy in registration and in giving change.

The safety factor of cash within our shops never hits you until you have been 'milked'. The exposed centre of the shop is too inviting. The drawer should always open *away* from public access.

There must be a strict rule for all sales assistants – never, NEVER leave the till open and go in search of change, nor leave for any other reason whatsoever without first closing the till. Shout for help yes, or better still have installed a small and inconspicuous alert button so that management can come to the rescue upon hearing an alarm.

An elementary point so often overlooked – keep a modest bank of small change somewhere on the premises so that your senior staff can bring it into use as required. If you employ no full-time cashier, your senior florist and/or salesperson should be responsible.

The cash register should be sited adjoining, or in the locality of the shop packing area. There are reasons for this which we will examine below.

Wrapping and packing area

When there is sufficient space behind the shop, most packaging and dispatch of orders can take place without interfering seriously with the pattern of work in the sales area. Such an arrangement is even more necessary at peak periods.

Nevertheless, one must always allow for easy access to stock, the bulk of which may be displayed in the shop. Within the shop it is usual for packaging to be carried out under the eyes of the customer. In normal circumstances this gives opportunity for further discussion and perhaps an additional sale, whilst the customer is visually assured that all that he or she has purchased is within the parcel. Lack of space can be a problem in a small shop. The packing of one customer's goods should not impede or get in the way of the next customer, hence, if sufficient space can be made available, a packing unit is desirable in the sales area. Make sure, however, that sales staff have sufficient space in which to operate. A properly fitted unit, with everything to hand, will save valuable time and encourage careful handling of produce. Have more than one roll of wrapping paper in use, plus plenty of auxillary wrappings of the kind required in your business, ie tissues, corsage boxes or bags, absorbent paper, tying materials, tapes and/or string, reel wire, scissors, adhesive tape and staplers. All of these are essential, so do not be mean. Have at least two of each item so that there is no loss of time in waiting for, say, the one pair of scissors. Better still, equip each of your sales staff with certain essential tools such as scissors and a knife.

As with the cash register, staff access to a packing area should be easy and should *flow*. Never site in a cul-de-sac, as this will inevitably produce congestion and strained tempers.

Access and movement

Access routes between shop, workroom and storage areas should be wide and high enough to give ease of movement to all persons using those rooms, and to avoid damage to stock being carried. Swing doors are a menace unless they can be secured in an open position with one's foot. All service doors should have a look-through panel to avoid collisions. The cost of this amenity is small compared with the cost of shattered flowers, vases and bruised limbs. (When space permits, management might introduce a one-way traffic system as a safety measure. If busy restaurants can use the system, why not the florist?)

Keep lines of approach clear on both sides of the doors. Never site working benches or packing areas in a corridor. You may infringe fire regulations if you do, and you will, in any case, create delays and inconvenience your staff.

The above sounds so elementary, but all too often we cherish these expensive inconveniences for too long.

Oil on the wheels

In siting, or re-siting, the key points in the shop, give some thought to the amount of movement that is going to be necessary between them. Distances to be covered and points of high traffic density.

In an average shop transaction the salesperson will be required to make at least six separate moves:

1 To the sales area, plus some walking around with the customer
2 From sales area to packing unit
3 From packing unit to customer
4 From customer to cash control
5 From cash control to customer
6 To base or the next customer

No great distances are involved in a small shop, but the congestion risk can be great. In our larger store it is expected that a greater volume of sales will be taking place, distances will increase, but congestion should be easier to avoid. So, in either case:

1 Study where the lines of communication cross and, if they must, make sure it is where there is room for manoeuvre, NOT in a narrow corridor and not at a blind corner.
2 Open up reasonable but not exessive distances between the key points. If they are all crammed together in a small area they will create their own congestion.
3 There are advantages to be gained if cash control and packing areas adjoin but it must still be easy for staff to move quickly to and from either place. A compact display of small accessories for the flower arrangers can be situated close to the till. This is a good position from which to obtain extra sales.

At this stage you may well have decided that you are unable

physically to make more than one or two adjustments. But, for the well-being of yourself and your staff, be willing to experiment and adapt. Even one re-adjustment may save you both time and money. Further, no adjustment need be permanent.

The immovable objects

Premises, perhaps because of their age or some long-past adjustment to business purposes, can have problems which are relatively immovable. We can, in fact, be laid flat on our faces by some architectural idiosyncrasy of the place in which we run our business. Yet we recognise that a move to new premises or a complete de-gutting can be very expensive.

But we can still fall flat on our faces. So can our sales staff. Read from a USA trade report:

> 'Stairway injuries. According to recently published data from the US Government, approximately 56,000 injuries occur annually involving stairs, ramps and landings. Aside from weather conditions, the leading causes are: poor lighting, condition of stairs, obstacles on stairs, condition of railings and that of the walking surface.'

Your staff will need to move swiftly and safely, to and from any point within your premises. The swifter and more safely they move, the more economic they will become to you as employees. Also, they may live longer!

Starting with **stairs**, it is a fact that in a proportion of our stores, especially in crowded city sites, at least one or two stairways have to be negotiated as part of the normal duties of our staff. Parcels, vases, flowers, arrangements and plants are transported from one level to another as a daily routine. So check the following points:

Lighting – all too often poor and, where the walls are dingy, utterly inadequate for safe movement.

Condition – treads get worn, covering becomes tatty – all too easy to ignore until someone trips.

Obstacles – yes, 'Stick it on the stairs and I will take it up next time'. Another disaster!

ACCESS TO COOLER
AND STORE ROOM

ORDER DEPARTMENT
PACKING & SOME DISPLAY

SHELF DISPLAY

EXTERIOR
DISPLAY
OF PLANTS
AND
SHRUBS
This is an
area which
can be
enclosed by
gates at night,
but giving
access to
workroom
and cooler to
rear of shop.

DISPLAY

OVERHEAD ARCH – AN IMPLIED DIVISION

DISPLAY

CUT FLOWER
DISPLAY

MAIN DOOR

DISPLAY

DISPLAY

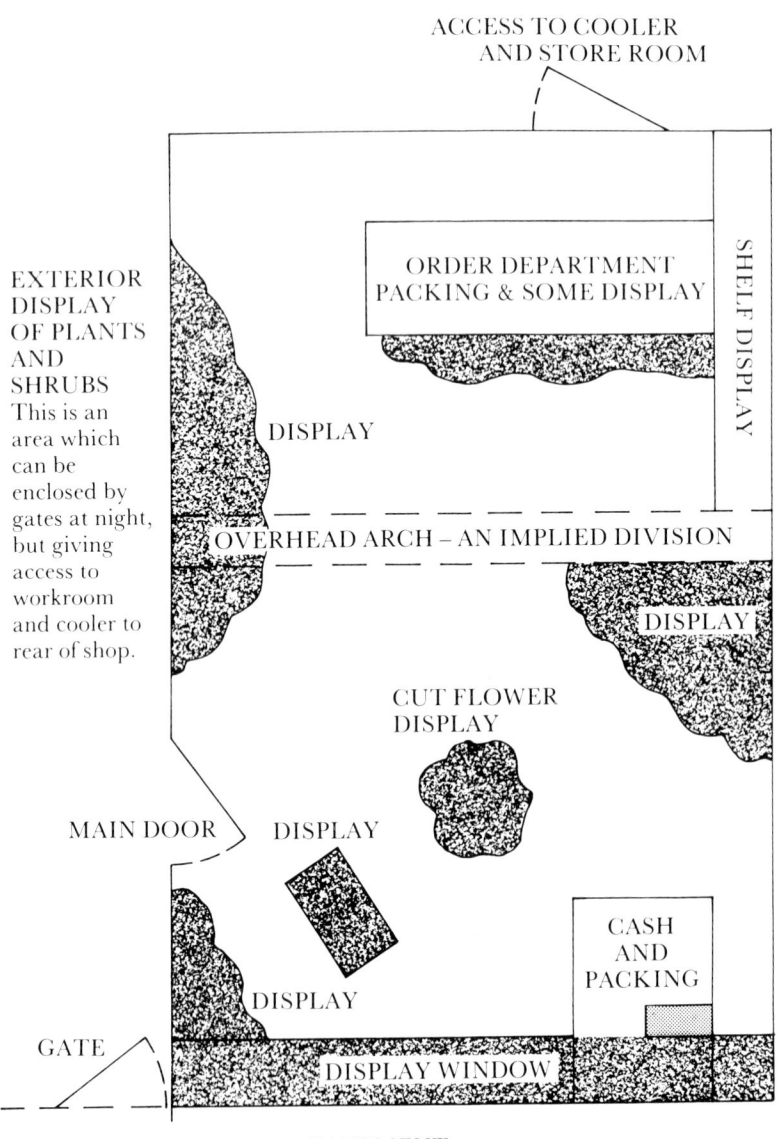

CASH
AND
PACKING

GATE

DISPLAY WINDOW

PAVEMENT

◀ A fully equipped workroom is at the rear and is not shown on this diagram.

Pavement outside the shop is very narrow, hence the value of side entrance, approached through an attractive display of outdoor plants.

Frontage is about 5.5 m and depth about 9 m. A high arch implies some separation within the shop.

Note particularly the site of essential features – all are non-fixture and can be adjusted seasonally.

A cooling cabinet (not shown) serves two shops

Railings – usually sufficient, but should be checked for safety.
Surfaces – non-slip, please, and with edges whitened.

The same kind of survey should be made of all walking surfaces. No doubt your floor is perfect. (Is it? Have a look in the passages, doorways and corridors.)

Floor conditions deteriorate and all too often are tolerated until there is an accident. Loose or cracked surface tiles, threadbare covering, dampness, puddles. If you have any of these, put them right – NOW.

Lighting is often suspect, and the minimal is not good enough. Skylights, too, are fine until it gets dark outside.

Obstacles – empty vases, surplus stock, unsaleable flowers, boxes, pots, all are hazards. There must be a strict drill with your staff against 'dumping' the unwanted object.

If there is a threshold, make sure that it has some positive function other than as a hurdle and trip-wire; if possible, get it removed.

Doors should not open out on to a corridor and, if you can, replace hinged doors with sliding doors; you will save space and time.

One other place full of hazards is the **sink**. Taps should be high enough so that the tallest stock vases can be filled. There should be a hot water supply as well as cold. Two sinks are better than one, and should have wide outlets. Plastic or rubber mats in the sinks will reduce damage to valuable pottery. Draining boards should incline slightly (not steeply) towards the sink (and NOT towards the shoes of the user).

Taps and outlets should be kept in good order, and if you have a

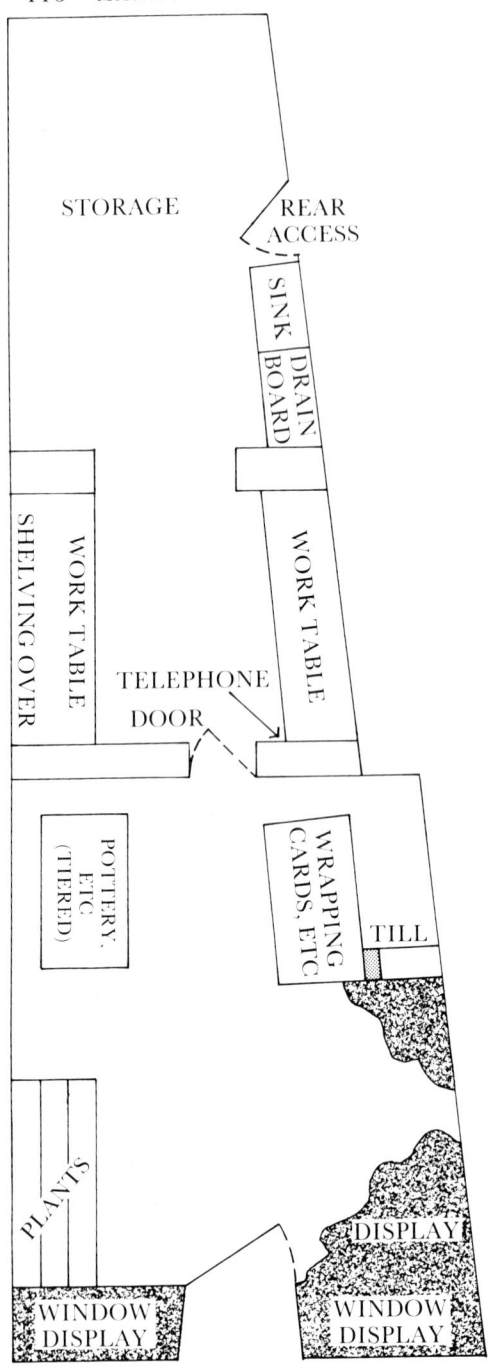

This is an interesting and very clever use of premises that have peculiar shape.

The frontage is about 4.5 m over all, and the site tapers to less than 2 m at the extreme rear of the storeroom.

There is rear access to a small yard, but no natural lighting in either shop or workroom, so there is a cunning use of fluorescent lighting and filament spotlights.

The display areas are adjustable in size and are tiered for maximum effect.

This is a small shop, but full use has been made of every cm of space, and the key-points, till and telephone, are situated safely and giving the proprietor full view of them whilst they are being used.

The window bed is raised, to conform with surrounding premises, but with narrow pavement outside this makes for easy viewing and safety.

The shop faces a busy small-town High Street and is surrounded by principal Banks and commodity shops. An ideal situation flooring problem anywhere, it will be near the water supply because of the unavoidable splashing that will occur. Check for puddles, safe surfacing and waste disposal. A sack of soggy stems and foliage will contaminate the room, and create dangerous working conditions. There must be a mandatory clearing-up drill, and a duty rota is preferable to leaving it always to the same unfortunate 'junior'.

These are but a few of the flashpoints. Again we hear the cry, 'This is all too elementary' – but have *you* looked? (See also Appendix page 147).

Documentation

Another aspect of the work of our sales force relates to documentation, and it is worthwhile taking a long hard look at the systems we are using.

Many of us, over recent years, will have adapted to one or other of the commercially supplied systems, and it would serve no good purpose to upset something to which much care and thought has been given. However, many florists are still out of date, to say the least. Many are using systems that, like 'Topsy', have grown over a number of years and possess self-created backwaters of unnecessary documentation and wastage of time.

With any order we need to keep in mind the objectives: the uses, and end products of documentation. We know that we must keep adequate records for taxation and VAT purposes. We need, also, to be able to refer back if and when a complaint arises or a query upon the nature of any order. These are essential records; usually *one* filed copy of every order is sufficient.

If you find that you are giving storage space to two or three copies of every past order, there is something wrong with your system. Maybe someone is doing much more writing than is necessary, maybe you are buying far more paper than you need.

Every order will be for either cash or credit. Your customer will need a receipt if it is in cash, or an invoice if it is credit. You need a copy of the order so that you can carry it out properly and that copy should be filed upon completion so that you can refer to it for any reason. Additionally, for all credit business, you need a copy for your account system. Both workroom and accounting systems must be

118   MANAGEMENT

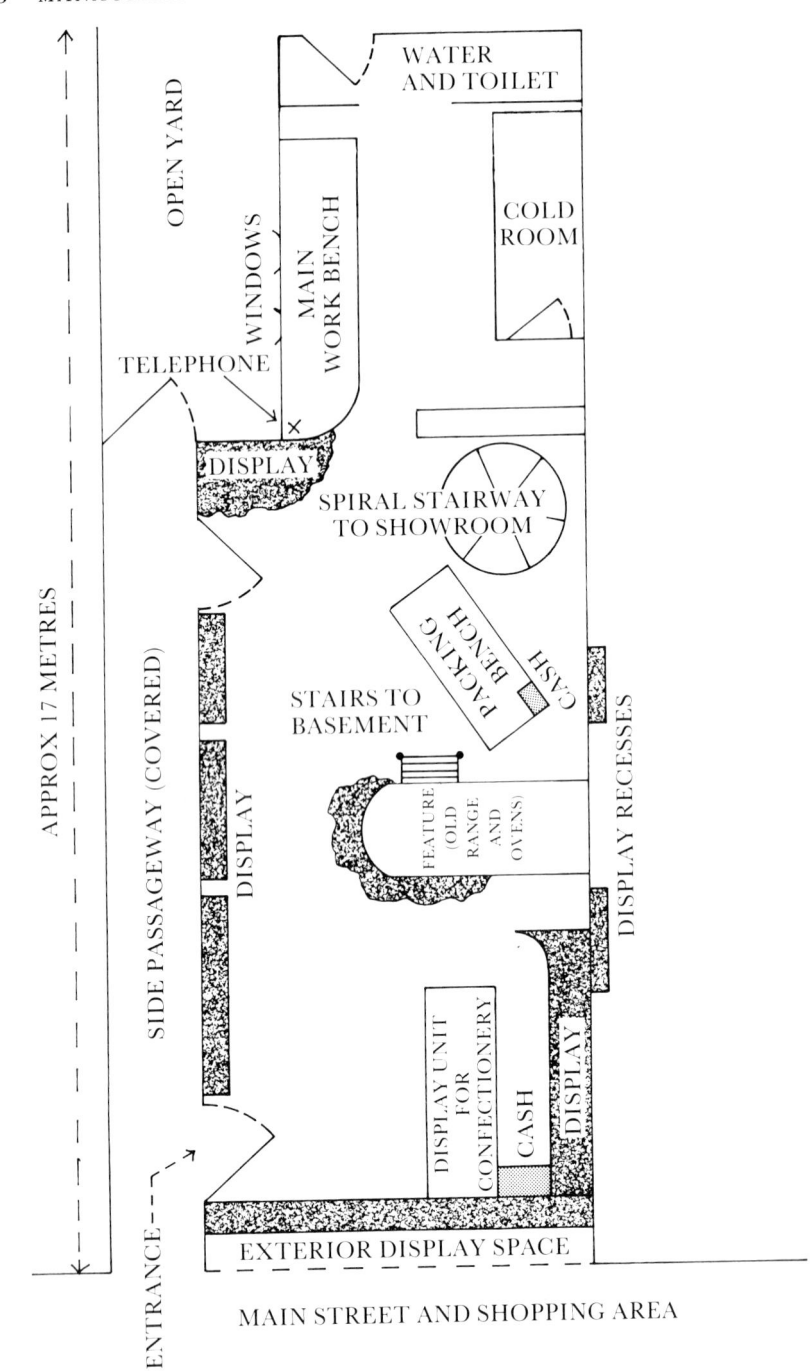

Floor Plan

- OPEN YARD
- WATER AND TOILET
- WINDOWS
- MAIN WORK BENCH
- COLD ROOM
- TELEPHONE
- DISPLAY
- SPIRAL STAIRWAY TO SHOWROOM
- PACKING BENCH
- CASH
- STAIRS TO BASEMENT
- DISPLAY RECESSES
- FEATURE (OLD RANGE AND OVENS)
- DISPLAY
- SIDE PASSAGEWAY (COVERED)
- APPROX 17 METRES
- DISPLAY UNIT FOR CONFECTIONERY
- CASH
- DISPLAY
- ENTRANCE
- EXTERIOR DISPLAY SPACE
- MAIN STREET AND SHOPPING AREA

◀ This shop is situated in a small but beautiful provincial city which was once a Roman settlement. Many of the buildings are 'listed' properties, and the proprietors of this flower shop were thus unable to alter the structure, or interfere with the internal design of the building. Add to that its depth, the narrow frontage, and there were real problems.

These problems have been overcome, first by making sensible use of every centimetre of space, and secondly by turning the immovable features of the building to an advantage. For example, the great stone fireplace and ovens once part of a wall separating two sections of the shop, are now a perfect setting for the display which surrounds the weathered stone.

Visibility is good from end to end of the relatively narrow premises and, apart from the above 'feature', every piece of equipment and furnishing is moveable. The cash tills are sited in safe places. Display recesses and shelving make full use of all wall space. Lighting is good throughout in spite of low ceilings and, to the passer by, the shop has the look of a treasure cave, full of flowers and smiling people.

The basement is used partly for storage and partly as a transmission and receiving point for relay orders. Modern equipment has taken the strain, and one member of staff can cope easily, even at peak periods.

The spiral stairway leads to the upper floors: a showroom for dried and fabric flowers and arrangements, a second workbench for peak period working and an office for the 'boss'. Above, on the second floor there is further storage and a well-equipped staffroom. A chair for everyone, washing and cooking facilities, a refrigerator, oven, and individual lockers for each member.

Looking at this successful conversion, one message is very clear: listed premises, even those with apparently many problems, can be turned to advantage. Flowers, displayed against the stonework of a very old building can look even more attractive. What is more, the building is being preserved, usefully.

---

efficient and inter-related, but not productive of multiple copies of the same order. At the end, when the deal is completed, and the account settled, you need to file but one copy.

From the viewpoint of the sales floor (and this is the area towards which all these suggestions are attuned) there are no complications in booking orders on to a triplicate pad. Avoid any necessity for any re-copying of orders; indeed the only place where this may be necessary is in the accounts office. A photocopy will eliminate the possibility of any error. Nevertheless, the old daily order book still exists in many places; often nobody is quite sure why it is used or who looks at it, and it is a prime area for wastage of time and creation of mistakes.

Check your systems to ensure that there is a *good* reason for *any* manual copy writing. Also, have a look at your records store; if there is duplication, you need to re-think your methods.

In order that your sales staff can operate economically, with the minimum of irritation and delay, be sure that your order forms are:

1 Large enough, and carry the necessary promptings for the main details of an order. (If the pad is too small, mistakes are inevitable, bad writing is encouraged and extension onto continuation sheets simply multiplies the risks.)
2 Bound in strong but light-weight supporting backs, or covers. Metal dispensers may be preferred, but tend to be heavy and not very easy to hold. Comfort in writing is necessary if you expect legible writing.
3 Printed on paper of sufficient quality to stand up to the use of a ball-point pen, and at a later stage to withstand dampness without disintegration. Cheap re-constituted paper, looking rather like dried porridge, is fragile and dangerous.

Suggested format for a counter order form (opposite)

The flower relay organisations supply specially designed order pads for relay work. This form is intended mainly for orders which you will carry out from your own premises, but is suitable also for the initial booking of relay orders. It is especially useful beside the telephone as it carries reminders of all information which is essential for the completion of the order and for your records. (Sequence of information may be adjusted to suit your system.)

Order form pads are also available from stationery suppliers to the trade.

MANAGEMENT 121

Your trading name, address, telephone number and relay insigna	**FLORIST**
Destination of order	Day, date and time .... Name .... Address ....
Nature of order	Goods (or flowers) ....
Card	Card ....

Customer details and costings

Customer	Goods	
Name	Delivery	
Address	Relay	
....	Telephone	
....	VAT	
Paid/To pay	Total	
Day, date and time		

Accounting details – delete as necessary

If filed with a clip at the top, the execution details, day, date and time may be repeated here

Peaks and bottlenecks

Peak selling periods are welcomed throughout the flower industry, for the business they bring and for the numbers of the public who come into our shops perhaps for the first time. The opportunities are legion – can we grasp them?

If things are to go well, we must handle a heavily increased volume of produce in a short and limited time. Staff must be prepared, temporaries brought in, and adjustments made to both layout and systems.

Temporary and part-time staff can be of immense help if instructed properly, and an utter drag upon proceedings if brought in without preparation. They must be made familiar with the produce they will be handling, prices, system of handling cash, packaging and dispatch. Full-time staff must be fully informed of the role they will be expected to play, and of the areas in which the extra help will be used. A short briefing session, with all staff present, is recommended, after which the experienced staff can be expected to instruct the recruits in the basic procedures within the shop.

Select your 'temporaries' carefully and devote time to their preparation for the work. (As a bonus, you may sometimes pick up a potentially good full-time salesperson from a handful of 'temps'.) Make sure that they are deployed where help is really needed, that they are under the eyes of your full-timers and not (as has been known) relegated to some menial job such as clearing up empty boxes in a rear store, a job which could well have waited until after the peak.

Ensure also that the essential work is carried out fairly and that people are directed with tact and understanding. Clashes of personality, age or temperament must be avoided. (They can turn a peak period into an employer's nightmare.) Generally, those with temperamental problems should not be engaged in selling duties – certainly not when the pressure is on.

The peak period will usually require the provision of extra space for packaging and for writing out orders. Space for, and ready access to the cash register or cash desk should be studied and enlarged as necessary. Careful planning will avoid the situations in which sales staff are falling over each other in one place whilst another part of the shop is not fully used.

It should be remembered that the public, when waiting to be served, will gravitate towards any packaging area that can be identified. If you have only *one* place you may well find that you have a line of customers waiting to be served at one side and another line of assistants waiting to pack up flowers at the other. A typical bottle-neck. Possibly a good picture to contemplate, but very costly in terms of wasted time and lost customers. Convenient conditions for every operation should be sought at peak periods and at all other times. (Refer back to pages 110 and 111.)

Where space is limited, the packing and dispatch of a large number of orders can seriously disrupt service to the shop customers. This must not be allowed to happen, and it may become necessary to utilise some other parts of the premises not normally used for shop purposes. Turn, perhaps an empty garage into a temporary 'pack and dispatch' department. Others in similar circumstances have found it necessary to hire some nearby empty store or warehouse for a few days. In either case, make one of your trusted regular staff responsible for its effectiveness and smooth running. Benches have to be erected and stock, containers and all packing materials must be transported and arranged ready for use. Allow sufficient staff so that there is a smooth progression of work without too much expensive overtime. Make sure too that your van driver can cope with the deliveries. If in doubt, use extra transport or make use of a local delivery service.

Relay systems can seem complicated and it is unwise to expect temporary staff to absorb procedures in a short time. Thus it is likely that most relay order sending will be in the hands of the full-time sales personnel. But the problems do not end there, because in a busy shop there may be competition for the use of the telephones or other relay equipment* and at such periods every other florist is likely to be equally 'busy'. So there are delays in getting calls through. A temporary extra line or lines will help to clear your outgoing business and leave your regular listed lines open for incoming business. Even the use of a private line, say from your own residence, will relieve the pressure. Relay systems *must* operate as efficiently as throughout the

* The Messenger system (see page 89) can eliminate much of this problem.

rest of the year. Indeed, it is even more important, for peak periods bring in the non-regular shoppers, people who possibly have never used the relay service before.

The 'phone will be under pressure also from your customers, emphasising again the need to use your extra lines for all *outgoing* calls and to allow the business to get in to you on your listed lines. However, telephones must be manned, and as with sales staff, you will be wise to bring in temporary help. Make sure, however, that you employ only intelligent people who are familiar with telephone procedures. Students on vacation from business training are most adaptable for this kind of work, though older folk with business and telephone experience are equally helpful. Do not economise by under-manning your communication system – your trained sales personnel are wasted if required to undertake prolonged periods of telephone duty when they should be selling.

One other duty which falls firmly upon management is to organise proper refreshment breaks for all staff. People working at high pressure burn up a lot of energy. Some get over-enthusiastic and imagine that they are indestructable. Meal and coffee breaks are utterly essential and should be arranged so that you do not lose the services of all your top sales personnel at the same time. Special rotas should be drawn up and the lunch-time break can sometimes be covered by overlapping part-time shifts.

Good staff relations are never wasted – they radiate back through your sales staff to your customers.

Note
Much that has been said in the preceeding chapters is based upon the likely problems to be encountered in average, fairly large shops. Similar situations can exist in any sized flower shop. Scaled down, or scaled up, such problems can occur. Your solutions may differ from ours, but your attention to the smooth running of your shop is an all-time managerial responsibility. A few answers have been suggested, a few possible solutions that may be applicable, but you may well have better ideas.

Planning for the peak

Here is a critical path analysis for a typical peak period – Christmas. It is wise to have similar work-plans for other peaks during the year, such as St Valentine's Day and for Mothering Sunday. (Remember that dates change every year for the latter.)

You need to plan for Christmas trading and not just let it happen. Early in December take a very critical look at your display and selling space. Store, out of sight, any unessential goods – it is amazing how one can become accustomed to seeing items which have no significant sales value in the winter months – aerosol, sprays, vases of dried grasses and foliages, a box of used flower pots at 'special' price, and even one or two plants that have seen happier days. Put these cherished items away for Christmas and give yourself space for the increased business that is there for the asking. Do you need to move, or adjust any of your display units? Do you need any additional shelving or tables? Some modest re-siting of units can be of benefit for this short period, and a change of aspect will often excite the interest of the public.

The following is a suggested *Christmas Planner*. The dates are adjustable to your local conditions, but are approximately right and will serve as reminders.

DECEMBER

1 Check your transport vehicles and have them serviced as necessary. Even your own car, for you never know when you may need it in a hurry.
 Check stocks of sundries, particularly wrapping paper, bags and carriers, string and (if used) ribbons.
 Check your shop lighting and get some reserve tubes or bulbs into store (a tube 'on the blink' can drive one to distraction on a busy day)
 Decide if you will need any extra staff over the Christmas period, and if you do, start looking. Staff may be easier to obtain today, but the inexperienced still need some basic instruction.

7 Complete any change round of display and bring in a reasonable

range of seasonable plants: solanums, kalanchoes, primulas, growing bulbs, cyclamen, begonias and one or two poinsettias to complete the seasonable touch.

If you are offering dried or artificial decorations, they should be already on display. If you intend to handle foliages, holly wreaths and Christmas trees, these also should be displayed. Ensure that you have sufficient space for these items.

12/14   Make sure that your office work is up to date and that you will not be called away from more essential work to answer correspondence or pay bills during Christmas week.

15/16   Bring in your extra staff, and brief them as to their duties. Make sure that you put your existing staff into the picture.

If not done so already, make one of your regular staff responsible for the flowers and plants display.

16/17   Receive delivery of main batch of plants.

Service and display them for fullest possible impact.

19   Main deliveries of cut flowers should be arriving now. Deliveries can be spred over two/three days. It is assumed that you will have been selling flowers throughout the month, but this is the period of peak display.

20/24   The last five days of Christmas week are the period of peak sales. The actual peak varies from year to year, but it is usually reached on 22/23. Do not worry too much about the 24th, and if you can see a few gaps on the 23rd, leave them, for it is far better to sell out than to have to cope with over stock.

25   If you are open on Christmas Day, be prepared to sell quite a few plants and flowers. You can fill a need when many florists are shut, and many people like to buy flowers for their hosts when on their way to the Christmas family party.

28/29   *After* Christmas, sit down quietly and save yourself a lot of worry next year. It is surprising how much detail can be forgotten in twelve months, and a written record is invaluable. It need not be long.

Simply record:
– the varieties, quantities and prices of the flowers and plants you bought
– when, and how delivered and their general condition

- their selling prices and any wastage by 'marking-down-to-clear'
- staff: any extras employed, for how long and for how much
- weather: what it was like and how it affected your trading
- any other happenings that could have influenced business. Things that might have gone better and the things that went well.

Next December you will either pass upon yourself a vote of 'thanks' or one of 'no confidence!'

Buying

Changes have taken place and are still taking place in flower production and distribution. The tragic disappearance of so many sources of supply in Britain and the continually growing influence of the Dutch markets are major factors. The situation is still somewhat fluid and the full effects of this dramatic change are yet to be seen.

Factually, however, fewer retailers are now buying directly from our markets in Britain. Those who opt out are buying their supplies from travelling wholesalers who may be obtaining their supplies through our markets here or, more often, bringing van-loads of flowers directly from Aalsmeer. Florists situated a long way from a market, and off the main-line rail services may have no choice. Others, more centrally situated can choose, and maybe get, the best of both worlds.

Arguments rage about the long-term results of this intrusion into our established market system. But back in the retailer's shop the basic needs are unchanged. The retailer must somehow get the flowers that he needs, of the required quality, at a reasonable price and at the time he needs them. If by purchasing from one source or another – or even a combination of two or three sources – he can achieve this, he is buying well. In some instances there will be little choice, whereas in a market there may be a dozen wholesalers willing to serve him. Most vulnerable is the retailer with but one wholesaler willing to call. The service may still be good, but if you are in such a situation you would be wise to attend a market occasionally, even if it means a long journey, and perhaps establish contact with a reliable country-order wholesaler who will be willing to send supplies to your nearest station. Most important, do not lower your sights about quality, for however it comes and whatever it costs, it is cheaper than allowing your standards to drop. Continue to be discerning, critical and selective. Watch for danger signs whether you buy in a market or from the smart van outside your shop.

The condition in which flowers arrive with you is important. Too many of the flowers coming from abroad have spent too long in a cooler after harvesting. If you have a good relationship with your supplier he may advise – on the other hand he may not. Undue limpness of both flowers and foliage can be due to deliberate dry-packing, but is more likely to be the flowers' response to a prolonged period of cooling, and the condition may persist whatever you do. Stems can tell a story too. Spray chrysanthemums with 10 to 12 cm of saturated, slimy and sometimes brown stems have certainly had a long period off the plant. The flowers may look young, but they will not have a long life. With carnations, the flowers should be crisp. A gentle touch with your hand will tell you if they are, and if they are limp or flabby to the touch, they will probably disappoint by dying quite quickly.

For market work, a clip-board and buying sheet will be found most useful. The design suggested opposite may be varied to suit your personal requirements, but has it value in a number of instances. A buying list may be entered on the left-hand and purchases recorded on the right. The completed list can be filed and entered into the bought ledger later in the day, or at the end of the week.

The 'Wants' list
Computerised stock keeping is somewhat beyond the reach and the need of the average florist. Nevertheless, a 'wants' list should be part of the standard equipment. Even in a family run business, it is so easy to forget an impending shortage. You, or someone you entrust may have every intention of noting that you are starting the last box of foam, or binding tape or, even, that you are short of light bulbs. The pad can be held by a clip and hung, with a pencil, in some prominent place within the workroom of office.

MANAGEMENT 129

Your trading name
address and telephone number

Date .... Cash .... Buyer				
REQUIRED		BOUGHT		
		From	Variety/Price	Total

Increase to A4 size for practical usage

WANTS
VERY URGENT
STOCK RUNNING LOW
EQUIPMENT REPLACEMENTS

Plants which are offered in very dry condition are suspect, for their condition may be due to exposure to cold wind, either in transit or in a market. African violets are particularly tender and although the plant will stand up quite well for a day or so after a frost, the flowers quickly shrivel and tend to lose their colour.

Be discerning. Develop discernment and accept only that which meets your standards of quality. If you can, develop a touch for flowers. Impossible to define, the 'touch' is to do with instinct, an instinct that can develop with experience and, above all, a liking for handling flowers.

Beware of clearance offers. Not all are bad, but there is usually a reason for such offers to be made. Always see what you intend to buy, and think carefully: Why is this being offered? Can you sell it? Is there time to sell it? Offers made on Christmas Eve, when you may be flushed with a week of good trading can seem very tempting. But Christmas trade tends to fall off suddenly, especially on Christmas Eve, so be careful.

If you are not happy with the choice of flowers being offered, consider buying directly from Holland. There are a number of firms there who specialise in direct sales.

The Trade Press is a vital link between the retailer and the rest of the industry. Not everything printed is of necessity of vital interest to you, but no proprietor or manager can afford to be an 'island'. What happens in the rest of the industry can affect you, and your buying problems can often be answered by the information and advertisements carried in such monthly publications as the *Flower Trades Journal*[1] and *The Florist*.[2]

Direct contact with other retailers is immensely valuable, too. Both relay organisations arrange meetings from time to time, giving opportunities for public discussion of trade matters and direct conversations with those who may be working in conditions similar to your own. Buying problems and their solutions are the subject of many a casual meeting over tea, or even something stronger. Whenever possible, take your staff along too – one alert youngster

[1] *The Florist*, 120 Lower Ham Road, Kingston-on-Thames, Surrey
[2] *The Flower Trades Journal*, 17 Wickham Road, Beckenham, Kent

can possibly pick up information that could be of vital interest to you, especially in the area of stock, and buying procedures.

One final question on buying. Is your stock influenced by personal preferences? If it is, are you allowing your personal likes and dislikes to over-rule the needs of your business?

The question is included because, in the face of a chorus of denials, it has happened and will continue to happen.

Certainly the shop should have your personal touch, perhaps even your personal image, but to persist in the face of reduced profits, and heavy waste is dangerous. Care, in compiling a buying list, will control the personal impulses – after all, we are in business to make a profit.

Marketing, publicity and advertising

A great deal to cram into one chapter, but they are all related. 'Shop-keeping' is a comfortable term, implying a fair return for your labour and a comfortable state of mind. In today's world, the brutal facts are that comfort in business has to be fought for and earned. Nobody can afford to 'keep a shop'; rather, the shop coupled with your efforts, must be keeping you. The shop is your field, vantage point, stage and backcloth. Within it, and from it, you have to earn your living.

You achieve this by buying and selling. Experts may call it merchandising or marketing. Whatever you call it, you are the architect of its success. You are also the builder, quantity surveyor, works manager, operator and financier. If it goes wrong, *you* carry the can!

The spur or driving force comes from your marketing policy. Marketing means, in essence, the control of the product from its manufacture, through distribution to its eventual sale – its prime cost, eventual price to the public, promotion and significance as a profitable item. Also, to recognise in good time that the day will come when it will be overtaken or replaced by other products. Thus, marketing means full control from beginning to end. As retailers of a product which is very largely grown by others, distributed by others, our control is very limited. A few of us may have manufacturing interests and a few others actually grow plants and flowers. Should we, then, forget the term 'marketing' altogether? Not entirely, for its philosophy has so many elements of truth which can be adapted for our operations.

Sometimes we are tempted to leap into advertising, regarding it as a kind of life-line. But advertising, when neither purpose nor objective is clear is seldom any use.

Advertising (which is a facet of marketing) must convey an image of your business and of that which you wish to sell. For example, you specialise in wedding floristry and you also sell flowers from buckets outside your shop on Saturdays, which do you advertise? Obviously your wedding speciality, for nobody is likely to come specially to buy a bunch of flowers from your buckets. (Yet the reverse could apply if you were running an entirely cash-and-carry business.) The key is to *know* what you wish to sell and to *know* your public.

Here are some questions which you should apply to yourself. Think, for a moment of your shop as if it were a product. Or maybe a brand of goods, to be nurtured, developed and protected against competition. Think of your shop design and impact rather as a manufacturer thinks of a package for his goods.

Consider:
Does it reflect the desirability of the contents?
Is the name prominently displayed? And is it memorable?
Does it describe effectively what you do and what you are selling?
Does your shop stand out in the shopping street the way some packages stand out on supermarket shelves?
Once the 'pack', ie your shop, is right, what about the prices? Are they competitive? If not, is there a real market opportunity for a premium priced product or service? And who will pay extra for that and what motivates them to do so?

Then ask yourself:
Are you dissatisfied with your turnover?
Are you losing out to competition?
Are most of your customers elderly? Do you need to begin to attract new, younger customers?

Are you prepared to make changes for the better in your public image?

If you have a '*Yes*' answer to any of these, you have a *prima facie* case for considering advertising.

Above all and like any other marketing director, YOU must yourself be totally convinced that what you offer your customers is as close as you can make it to what they will want or need to buy. Because only then is there any chance that your advertising will truly prove to be an investment from which you will get a proper return: *otherwise it is just another cost*!

Advertising is necessary if you are to bring public notice to new offers, new produce and new services. It is often necessary too in order to bring the shop into prominence at Christmas, Mothering Sunday, etc, the peak times when rivals in other industries can steal so much of your turnover.

You may also be expected to yield occasionally to benign blackmail and to support with advertising, local fetes, and church magazines. This is an exercise in public relations rather than advertising and you should accompany it with an offer of a bouquet for a visiting celebrity or maybe a prize for some competition or athletic event. Make sure your name goes with it on the programme, however.

In general, choose your media with care. Use a newspaper which is likely to be seen by your potential customers and ignore the rest. Be cautious about stunts or 'special pages' in which, if you are not careful, you will find your panel squeezed into a corner and almost obliterated by some nationally backed announcement.

Never buy advertising from unknown sources and always see a pull of your announcement before it goes out. Most retailers and small businesses are dependent upon a local rather than a national clientelle. Nation-wide marketing and/or advertising may not be right for you unless it is backed financially by a promoter. Isolated boosts and one-off specials have little lasting effect and are but one tiny facet of marketing.

Public relations

If, as a successful trader, your name is good in your town then your public relations have succeeded. But, how? As a person, your very influence within your shop will be noticed. Your ability to converse easily and effectively with salesmen, friends and customers, your attitude to your staff and to your neighbours in trade. But it does not stop with those who come into your shop. You need to be known in your town – perhaps in your local Chamber of Commerce – and, if invited, you should take up membership of an organisation such as Rotary or Soroptomists (for ladies). Support local events. These items will cost very little compared with direct advertising costs, whilst putting your name before a large number of people. But perhaps the best goodwill is built up through the quality and range of your stock.

The product

Quality

The quality must be of the highest within the potential sales bracket. In broad terms, this means that with *your* knowledge of *your* products and of *your* sales area, you must give thought to the type, grade and price range of goods that your potential customers will buy. Look also at the goods that they are buying elsewhere and which you would like them to buy from you. The goods that represent good value for money.

The supermarket for example, has a line of glassware very applicable to your trade. Do you stock it, or anything of comparable usefulness and value, or have they taken some of your potential business?

In floristry terms it is likely (though by no means the rule) that the highest grade of roses and carnations will find a readier sale in the prestige shopping areas than say, in a cash-and-carry store. But check this before arriving at hasty conclusions. That once designated 'working class area' may hold more trading potential than more prestigious places.

The highest quality within the bracket is stated but only you or a local adviser can determine the level and width of that bracket. Quality must compare favourably with rival products of a similar nature. For a business founded upon a 'quality' image, the thought of mass selling may seem abhorent; some sacrifice of standards of display may be necessary if additional sales are to be engendered, for example you may have to create more selling space.

In selecting a line to be marketed, care should be taken not to displace, or squeeze out, lines that are profitable. Rather, take a look at some unprofitable lines, some declining lines. You cannot afford to keep them as pets. Maybe your new promotions should replace them. Indeed, every healthy business should be steadily introducing new lines and new ideas to the public. And, equally steadily, eliminating those which no longer pay.

Availability and supply

If you are to promote an article (or a service) you must be sure that sufficient stocks are available for the initial reaction to your promotion and for continuity of supplies. 'Sold Out' might look good in your window, but it would have been better to have kept on selling. The public do not like being asked to wait for a new consignment. The safe rule is to ensure availability. This is not so easy for the florist who, for all perishable stocks, is at the mercy of crops, seasons and markets but is not difficult, however, for the promotion of a service, such as flower relay.

Dry goods, giftware and ancillary lines rely upon proper arrangements with the suppliers or manufacturers. It is dangerous to spend much promotional energy upon 'special offers', 'one-off' and (never) 'job-lot' goods. Also, exercise some caution in accepting all the assurances of a newly created firm who may have to encounter unexpected teething troubles. A straight forward supply agreement with a known and established firm is the best basis for your own marketing promotion.

We are reminded that some florists either grow, or in some

instances, manufacture, specialist lines. The marketing of these can be all the more rewarding by being exclusive, but supplies of raw materials should be established.

Unit size, unit pack and unit price

These are inter-related factors and should be studied as a group. All three must conform to the dimensions of the 'bracket' that we have mentioned above. With the pre-packaged goods, size does not seem to matter unduly; one sees small children staggering under immense packets of breakfast cereal, and the cars outside the supermarkets seem to have adequate room.

For the florists it is not so easy. Our goods are not, as a rule, pre-packed. So if we are to sell a 'line' we must be sure that it can be packed, delivered or carried out easily without embarrassment. Loose paper, dripping stems and ungainly parcels are deterrents.

Give thought to the possibility of improved, or neater, packaging for flower arrangements, dish gardens, etc. Whilst you may deliver many of these directly to the recipient, could you not be missing some sales because they are not easily carried?

Price is a dominant factor. The marketed lines must be good value, and must be *seen* to be of good value to the purchaser. Equally, they must show a profit, and in arriving at a price for the article, the percentage of profit must be related to the *quantity* to be sold; the anticipated *rate of sales* and the *ease of selling*. If you can increase your turnover with a minimal increase in staff and overhead costs, prices can become more competitive. Normal profit margins are related to the standards of service offered and the prestige of the store. Yet, if lines are to be sold in competition with other outlets, profit margins may have to be lowered. In other words, slow-moving individual selling is replaced by faster moving and greater volume of sales.

Give thought to the nature and volume of potential customers you intend to attract. Where are the sales to come from, from what income group, what strata of public are you trying to attract? Make sure that the goods you intend to offer are either needed, or are so attractive that people will not be able to pass them by.

Think coolly about this and discuss ideas with your staff. The fact that you happen, personally, to like china rabbits with pink spots does not mean that they will be popular with anyone else in your town!

The potential field of sale

Every business has a potential selling area from which to attract its customers. Most business people treasure the conviction that they have it in the palm of their hands; that they know their selling area, their potential customers, what they like and what they will buy, but many of them are wrong. They are wrong if they have never taken a look at those parts of their town that are not yielding sales.

One good friend told me of his nearby town, 'You'll never sell plants there. They are dead from the neck up and have no interest'. We carried out a little experiment, and plants went like hot cakes. The interest and the potential customers *were* there. Perhaps we can all be a little too comfy in our beliefs.

Further, there is no guarantee that an area that has produced enough business in the past twenty years is going to do so for ever. Maybe already there are changes, and complacency could be fatal in the present economic situation. It is not necessary to employ expensive business consultants to find out what is happening in your town. Take a day off and walk around your local shopping area. Look at the people, how they are shopping, why and how they travel, how they spend their money. Look particularly at the shops that could be your rivals, the confectioners, the fancy goods, records and clothing stores, also the supermarket. Ask yourself have they got some of your business; how will you get it back?

You will not get it by aiming only at your comfortable cushion of regular customers. If you take note and act accordingly, you will be taking another step towards marketing. For that is what it is all about – *going out after sales*. You will need to find the answers to many of the questions we have posed above. You will need to act upon them. Above all, you cannot afford to be a commercial snob; if your area has changed and some of the best folk have moved away, make it your business to serve those that have taken their places – often they have more money anyway. And if your shopping area is improving, make sure that you improve with it by ordering better goods, in a better way, and eventually, maybe, in a better shop. Do not let your rivals cash in on all the plums.

Space may be a determining factor. If there is plenty, it may be wiser to concentrate upon expansion into the less perishable goods of our trade. A clear example is shown by those who have expanded into a garden centre business. If ever good marketing paid off, it is in this area. Yet, few of us have space for such a move unless we up sticks and take new premises. Maybe we should concentrate upon some diversification into ranges of goods that can be handled in a relatively small space. Giftware, small light furnishings, ceramics, glass ware, flower arrangement accessories, dried materials, yes, even the provision of proper facilities for taking relay orders. Innovations, under any of these headings and backed by research and determination can bring a new look and a new life to a business. But the basic principles of marketing must still be applied: care over the product, its price, its pack, its availability, its competitiveness, and finally, your staff.

Consultation with one's staff and colleagues is utterly essential. Large concerns set up a permanent 'committee' structure to assess new lines, the committee being drawn from internal heads of departments and advisers. In a shop this is hardly practicable, yet you need to know as much as possible about customer reaction. Further, your staff are people, citizens of your town, and they could know even more than you about the people who do not shop with you, and why.

However small your business, it is essential that you communicate. Tell your staff (even if there is only one) what you are going to do. Get their opinions and enlist them on your side, especially those engaged in selling. They too have a vested interest in the success of your business. Their jobs are at stake if you fail.

Two more related thoughts:
Have you a second-in-command? One who could take over for a few days if you were to be ill, or suffered an accident? If you have such a person – and every wise manager will have one in mind – do be sure to keep him or her fully informed of your policies and plans.

Everyone, including management, needs a holiday. Inasmuch as you are required to grant holidays with pay to your staff, so too should management plan for and take a reasonable break. There is no virtue in overworking, and there are no rewards for martyrdom in business.

Finance

Finally, here are some difficult questions to answer:

Are you getting a fair return for all your labour?
Are you getting a fair return upon your original investment?
Is your business a viable asset that can be offered for a reasonable price when you wish to retire?

If you can give a clear affirmative to all of these, you have no worries and need read no further.
If you are not entirely happy (and who is?) read on . . .

Inflation has rendered the values of 1970 totally unrealistic. Even if applied proportionally to 1988, they have little meaning because the flower industry itself has gone through some pretty agonising changes and is still changing. Furthermore, there were, in 1970, some inherent faults in our system. One may look back upon the relatively Utopian conditions of the late fifties and early sixties with the sure knowledge that they will not return. Today the stakes are higher, the profits must be higher and a business must have a higher market value. The yardstick we could use twenty years ago is now out of date.

The profits of a business are the only source of income for the proprietor. If that income is insufficient, there are three possible reasons:

1 Turnover is not keeping pace with overheads. It is flagging.
2 Overheads are too high. (Too many staff, too much transport, premises too large and costly?).
3 Mark-up is insufficient and is yielding too little gross profit.

If (1) above, is the case, it is hoped that the preceeding chapters will have sown some ideas.
If (2) some re-appraisal of your staff needs might be helpful, plus a hard look at your transport costs and the costs upon your premises.
If (3) check your buying methods. Are you paying too much for an easy life? *Then* check your mark-up. This is a problem that is not uncommon amongst florists and yet it is one about which most are loath to talk.

Gross profit, overheads and net profit

Gross profit comes directly from sales, less the actual cost of the produce sold. From your gross profit you must pay all of your overheads before you are able to see any net profit.

In the last two decades, overhead costs have risen far more sharply than the selling prices of flowers, so that a proportion which might have been, say, 20% of gross profit in 1970, has risen to perhaps 40%, or even more, today. The selling price of flowers has risen also, but is still well behind the national average for inflation over the same period.

This is the factor which can trap the retailer. He argues that it is bad enough to have to pay for and charge for the increased price of flowers, and he backs away from an increase in mark-up to pay for the inflating overheads. He argues that he may lose goodwill and overall trade if he does so. Yet, his gross profit is being eroded by circumstances quite outside his control. So, if your gross profit is insufficient, your mark-up may need some adjustment, upwards.

Mark-up

Much has been written about mark-up. Figures like 100%, 125%, 150% and more are often regarded with horror and indignation by some sections of both press and public. With some justice perhaps if the full facts are not known.

First, however, points of frequent misunderstanding must be clarified. 100% mark-up means 100% added to the cost price of the product. Thus, an item which cost £1 will be sold for £2. (Percentage mark-up is based upon the lower figure, the cost price.) However, the retailer is free to fix his selling margins, and he may opt for 100% or more according to his calculated needs.

Obligations under VAT do not affect in any way your need to obtain a reasonable gross profit. Investigation and experience have shown that the notional gross profit from any given mark-up can be eroded very significantly by the following factors:

The risk element   Flowers are perishable, and unlike articles which can stay in stock for perhaps months, they have a limited vase life and an even shorter shelf-life as saleable products. A conscientious retailer will never knowingly sell flowers or plants which, being past their best, will fail to give satisfaction to the customer. Yet the buyer for your firm must be adventurous within the limitations set by good judgment; to use instinct and experience in making decisions and to see, or try to see the likely volume and nature of trade for which he or she is buying. Nobody can be right every time, and there will be casualties for a variety of reasons. Those casualties are known as *waste*.

Shortages   A consignment of flowers may include a shortage which is physical (short count or counts) or one which is related to low or indifferent grading of the flowers. Either way the retailer may face a loss, in monetary terms or in time wasted arguing with the sender.

Damage in transit   An unavoidable risk in an industry which is handling a high proportion of delicate produce. Damage can be caused by careless handling or undue delay in transit. Again, the retailer may face a loss. Claims are difficult to pursue and very time-consuming.

Transport charges   are often forgotten when the price of a consignment is calculated.

The display obligation   A florist with no flowers on show will never sell any. Display – especially at weekends and closed periods is vitally necessary but costs money. True, flowers used for display might otherwise be wasted, but display is essential and in order to maintain it at proper level, saleable produce may have to be used.

The 100% mark-up looks, and is very fragile when the hard facts are taken into account. Maybe the prudent florist should be looking at mark-up in terms of 125 or 150%, or even higher. Which is a disturbing thought for a florist already in a competitive situation, but necessary, and workable if applied with discretion. Top quality flowers that are in demand must carry the load, or even a little more, whilst day to day trading, cash-and-carry perhaps, may be treated more gently. Much will depend upon the quantity likely to be sold in either bracket in a fair day's trading, and a sales analysis is absolutely necessary. The average must come out right, and if that can be held, the problem of too little gross profit can be eased.

If you fear that you are handing too much advantage to your competitor, the increases should be combined with an improvement in range and quality of stock and better display. One curious and helpful factor is that many of the public are tired of gimmicks and have become much more discerning of true quality. In many cases price seems to be of secondary consideration. This has been proved by the popularity of certain 'package' offers, by no means cheap, and the success of the 'one rose in a box' scheme.

Evaluation of workroom costs

There is another area in which many florists lag sadly behind, to their own discomfort. This is in the price at which they are prepared to offer made-up floral designs. Absurdly low minimum prices are still quoted in many areas, regardless of the labour costs involved.

Skilled labour is something for which the florist should pay. In a family concern it rarely has its true recognition. If you are your own skilled florist, do you calculate the cost of your labour and incorporate it into the cost of the design you have made? For every one who does, there are ten who do not.

If you are employing a skilled florist, that person should receive a fair rate of pay. It tends to vary from city centre to country situation, but figures such as £2, £2.50 and £3 per hour are not unusual and in certain circumstances can and should be considerably higher.

Whatever the cost, it should be charged as part of the cost of the design. Many firms charge a standard rate for labour, which is, in fact the skilled florist's wage plus a percentage. This system is in line with many other industries (engineering for example) the argument being that the employer guarantees the designer's wage, whereas the customer only uses the skills of the designer casually, ie when the bouquet or wreath is purchased.

Thus, a standard design, say a small wreath, may contain flowers, foliages and sundries to the value of £10 at retail price. But to sell it at that price is uneconomic because the 'workroom' or designing cost should be added, bringing the full retail price to perhaps £15. These are suggested figures, and may vary according to local circumstances. But we suggest that if you are to sell floral designs, you must make a realistic charge for the labour/skills involved.

A simpler kind of calculation used by many florists, is to deduct a proportion or percentage of the full retail price before the materials are selected. The result can be much the same and, using the same example the £15 tribute might take a third (or 33%) workroom cost, bringing it to £10 for actual materials used. (At 25% or a quarter, materials would be to a value of £11.25). Very much must depend upon the area which is served by the florist, the spending power and attitudes of the likely customers, the overheads and establishment costs which have to be covered. Local competition may be another factor, but little is gained by lowering ones prices. Better quality and better value for money are the more effective weapons. The public today *is* quality conscious and will seek quality even if it costs a bit more.

There is this further point, if you are going to be paid for your services as a floral designer, you have an obligation to give value for money. If you are prepared to offer good standards of floristry you will have no qualms nor worries over charging the right price. Quality is self-evident.

To conclude upon a vexed and sometimes contraversial subject, the way ahead for your shop is in your hands. If you are entirely happy with your business and its economic future you need do nothing. If not, spare some thought on its prospects for the coming years.

There is no specific formula that will meet every set of needs, no one answer except that you should be prepared to *think*. Rich florists are few and far between. But there are many florists who enjoy a reasonably comfortable standard of living. They work hard, some very hard indeed, and obtain considerable personal satisfaction from their efforts. Sheer pleasure from handling flowers helps a lot too.

Finally taking a broad and general view, it appears that the more successful florists are those who offer the highest quality in flowers, floristry, plants, sundries and services. But not, of necessity, at the lowest prices. Services offered and the whole image of the shop, seen through its staffing, display and management count for a great deal with the public, who are often prepared to pay a little more for the pleasure of shopping. Less happy are those who offer variable standards of produce, and are forced, perhaps by competition, to rely very much on a cash-and-carry turnover.

There is no single path to success. The complexity of situations in which florists operate is enormous. Every shop has its own set of conditions and although similarities exist, no two sets of circumstances are exactly the same. That which is right for one may be wrong for another. Wise proprietors and managers have to plot a path through a difficult and sometimes unknown terrain, and the purpose of this book has been to guide and, hopefully, to clear away some of the foggy patches. If but one idea works for you, you will not have wasted reading time.

Pension schemes

Recent enquiries indicate that at least one third of those who run their businesses on a self-employed basis have made no provision for retirement pension. The prudent ones can be assured of a reasonable provision for living whilst the less prudent may have to accept somewhat reduced standards. Or they may find it necessary to continue to work for years after normal retirement age has been reached. Some may enjoy the latter situation. Some even thrive upon it. But for those with health problems, (who can be sure of health in old age?) a cushion of income, in addition to the State pension, is an absolute necessity.

There are many differing schemes, tailored to various circumstances, and it is wise to consult a reputable insurance broker before making a decision. Even if you think that you are in no need of such cover, you would be unwise not to look at the possibilities.

APPENDIX

Safety in the shop

Premises

All premises open to the public, and this includes all shops, must conform with current legislation upon Public Safety. Provision must also be made for employees, their safety at work, and for reasonable conditions in which to work. Your local authority will be able to advise you and supply you with the appropriate literature. A fire brigade officer will be willing to inspect and advise you upon any fire hazards and, of particular importance to florists, your electrical installation, wiring and appliances should be checked by a qualified expert, or a representative of your Electricity Board.

All of the above is essential. But there is a great deal that you can do for yourself before the expert is called in. Here are some suggestions:

If you employ staff, there must be adequate toilet facilities, with hot and cold water for personal cleanliness.

A standard first-aid box must be maintained and kept in some obvious place. In practice it helps if one member of the staff can accept responsibility for its care and re-stocking as necessary. An 'accident' logbook should be kept so that any incident can be noted at once, with columns for name, date, time and nature of injury.

Built-in hazards

Hazards and accident spots:
Check your floor coverings for undue wear, or slippery when wet
Any stairways should be well lit at all times, with safe treads. Whitened
    edges will help prevent an accident.
Doors should open safely, inwards to a room wherever possible. In
    congested spots, a sliding door is often much safer. Swing doors should
    have a see-through panel.
Any steps, or sudden variations of floor level should be clearly indicated,
    with whitened edges to all steps.
Lighting should be at least adequate, and must never dazzle anyone.

Furnishing should be moveable, but strong. A collapsing chair has been known to bring a heavy claim for damages.

Outside blinds may be damaged by weather or vandals. If they are rendered dangerous to the public the liability is still yours, so check, daily if in doubt.

Fire hazards

Fire hazards are relatively few in a flower shop. Yet, accidents still happen. If your premises extend to more than one floor, you must arrange for appropriate fire escape routes. Windows may have to be enlarged, or re-fitted, and occasionally an outside escape ladder may have to be fitted. A rear exit to the shop is essential – it need not be onto a public way, but must provide an exit from your premises.

Smoke is often more of a killer than actual fire – remember that clean air is often to be found close to the floor.

A fire blanket and appropriate fire extinguisher(s) should always be at hand in some obvious place.

Electrical hazards

Quite apart from lighting and heating installations, florists use a number of electrical implements such as glue-guns, foam cutters, kettles and vacuum cleaners. Staff must be instructed as to their safe usage, and all plugs should be situated at waist level (NOT at floor level where they can so easily become drenched with water.) No switches or plugs should be close to any washing or vase-filling sinks, and the plugs and cables should all conform to the latest safety standards. Radiators must be fully enclosed and no open-barred fires are allowed. If in any doubt, consult a qualified expert.

General

The last person to leave the premises at the end of the day should check all switches in the 'off' position except those which control a time switch or minimal heating. Check also that no casual smoker has left a cigarette smouldering on some flammable surface.

Some of the materials that a florist may use or have in stock are flammable though not of necessity dangerous. Dry foam burns easily giving off evil-smelling smoke so store well away from any naked flame. Dried flowers and many of the fabric flowers are equally flammable, so handle and store with care.

Aerosol cans are dangerous if exposed to heat and/or direct sunshine. Store in a cool, shady place, never near to heat or source of heat and, when empty, throw away with the rubbish. Never put on a bonfire. Never pierce the can if it seems reluctant to yield up its contents.

Rubbish should be taken outside the premises, preferably in plastic sacks. Unavoidably there will be a considerable quantity of used cardboard containers, and these should be flattened and tied. (If there is a local salvage scheme operating the organisers may be pleased to collect these bundles.) Avoid piling empty cardboard containers outside your rear entrance – fires are known to have been started amongst such piles and have spread to the whole building.

The following materials, likely to be used or sold by florists, have an element of fire risk. Except where stated otherwise, **water** should be used to extinguish the fire, but should this occur in or around an electrical installation first make sure that the **current is switched OFF**, or better still disconnected.

Product	
Oasis and similar wet foams	Generally unwilling to ignite spontaneously. Will spit and shrivel when dowsed. Keep away from the fumes
Dry foam	Burns easily and quickly giving off black fumes. Do not inhale
Styrofoam	Will collapse as it burns, and melt or drip. Black fumes given off. Do not inhale
Cellophane	Will shrivel and melt before igniting
Acrylics	Will melt and drip like jam
Polypropylene	Will collapse, melt and drip
Fabrics and fabric flowers	Will generally burn easily. Nylon based fabrics may melt and give off black smoke

Continued overleaf . . .

Paper	Dry loose paper is very flammable and will blaze up. Closely packed paper and damp will smoulder and smoke. May continue to smoulder seemingly after the fire is put out
Dried flowers	Very flammable and will blaze up suddenly
Fertilizers	Smothering not always effective – use plenty of water. Sodium chlorate will sizzle like a firework and may explode. Keep well clear and do not attempt to move hot containers
Aerosols	Keep cool by misting with water. They may explode and then burn, according to contents. Cellulose paint burns fiercely and *foam* is more effective than water in such cases. Stand well clear whilst fighting this blaze.

Smoke is always dangerous to health. The black fumes given off by many synthetic materials are positively poisonous. Use a mask or damp cloth over mouth and nostrils in any such emergency.

Always call the Fire Brigade if you have reason to believe that you have a fire in the premises.

Make sure that everyone within the premises is alerted and can get out, at once.

(Acknowledgement to Mr Jack Gillett, FRPI, AMIBF, MITD, is made for the information on flammable materials given above)

Index

Accountant 17
Accounts 18
Achillea 46
Advent 51
Advertising 132
Agapanthus 50
Alstroemeria 35
Anemones 44
Antirrhinum 50
Aquilega 46
Artificial 57
Asters 45
Autumn 49

Bedding plants 56
Books 60
Bulbs 56
Buying 33, 127

Campanula 45
Cards 60, 95
Care cards 93
Carnations 35
Cash 96, 110
Christmas 51
Chrysanthemums 36, 45
Complaints 98
Cone wrap 94
Credit 96

Daffodils 42
Dahlias 50
Daily operations 30
Delphinium 46
Display 52, 103

Diversification 56, 60
Documentation 117
Doronicum 46
Dried flowers 57

Eremurus 50
Equipment 27
Equipment, electrical 148
Extremes 50

Finance 15, 140
Fire precautions 148
Floristry, selling 68, 78
Flower arrangement sundries 59
Flower relay systems 34
Freesia 38
Franchises 25
Funeral flowers 76

Gerbera 38
Gentian 50
Giftware 59
Gladioli 39
Glassware 58
Gross profit 20, 140
Gypsophila 46

Holly 51
Home trading 24
Honesty 46
Hyacinths 44

Insurance 29
In-store care 53
Iris 40

INDEX

Kiosk 25

Legal notices 29
Liatris 49
Lighting 105, 115
Lilies 40
Lily of the Valley 50
Location of shop 25
Lupins 47

Management 101
Marigolds 49
Marketing 132
Mark-up 18, 41
Mistletoe 51
Myosotis 50

Narcissi 42
National Diploma 13
National Examinations Board 13
Net profit 21

Orchids 50
Order pads 121

Quality product 135

Packaging 93, 110
Paeony 47
Peaks 122
Pinks 47
Plants 52, 88
Poisonous plants 53
Pottery 58
Premises 22, 26
Publicity 132, 135
Pyrethrum 47

Relay orders 78
Ribbons 59

Roses 41

Safety in the shop 147, 148
Sales area 106
Sales staff 61
Scabious 48
Sea Lavender 47
Second in command 139
Servicing flowers 84
Society of Floristry 14
Solomons Seal 48
Spring season 42
Staff 29
Statice 50
Stephanotis 50
Stock rotation 83
Summer season 45
Sweet peas 48
Sweet William 48

Telephone selling 80
Temperatures 50
Temporary staff 122
Toys 60
Trade Press 131
Trading accounts 15
Training 13
Tulips 43

Vase life 31, 84
VAT 16
Violets 44

Wedding orders 72
Welsh College 14
Wicker and cane products 58
Windows 103
Workroom costs 144
Wrapping 94

Zinnias 49